AN INQUISITIVE ENGLISHMAN
IN SOUTH AMERICA

D0885153

MARTIN HALLIWELL

MERLIN BOOKS LTD.
Braunton   **Devon**

ISBN 0 86303 227-3
Printed in England by Maslands Ltd., Tiverton, Devon

CONTENTS

ILLUSTRATIONS

INTRODUCTION

Why travel? Perhaps it is a curiosity and the excitement of wondering what is beyond the next hill which leads one on and on. A curiosity which once begun can lead you into extreme danger, hardship, poverty and joy.

With over forty countries and 50,000 kilometres of shoestring hitch-hiking behind me, there was still the most fascinating and varied continent of all left to see.

For six months and with only £400 to my name I hitch-hiked a total of 28,000 kilometres through a continent of contrast. Up the world's largest river, through the mightiest of jungles, across the driest desert, through fabled Inca lands and mountain cities, to strange islands where giant tortoises and penguins bask in equatorial sunshine.

But the vitality of travelling is in the assortment of people one meets. I try to remember some of these people through the multitude of humorous, extraordinary and sometimes tragic happenings *en route*.

Martin Halliwell

CHAPTER 1

DOESN'T ANYONE SPEAK ENGLISH?

Most people have a feeling of uncertainty when they set foot on a continent for the first time. I know I did when I stepped out of the plane at Rio de Janeiro airport in August 1976. Equipped with a small rucksack, four hundred pounds and a determination to see as much of South America as possible in six months, I could not help but wonder what I had let myself in for, mingled with a certain tingling excitement at all the possibilities which lay before me.

Once outside on the road at 9 a.m. GMT, but 5 a.m. Brazil time, I immediately became aware of my first limitation. I tried to ask in which direction the city was and how far away, but not being able to speak a single word of Portuguese or Spanish, I could not obtain a reply to even that simple question. Oh yes, everyone knew where I wanted to go, but they could not accept the fact that anyone should want to walk or hitch to Rio. There were plenty of people who could point out to me where the taxi stand was, but if you want to survive, you have to economise right from the start. It takes a little time to get accustomed to a new culture, to find out how things work in a strange country, in short, to find one's feet. Well that was my excuse to myself, when I changed 10 dollars with a stall keeper outside the airport (I did not want to change too much as I did not know the rate of exchange) and paid for a lift into the city.

I was glad I did not try to walk after all. The airport is many miles from the city and for a long time we seemed to be driving through an area of shanty towns which surround the city proper. There must be an awful lot of people who live in home-built huts of corrugated iron, wooden boards and concrete, on the outskirts of Rio. They are to be seen all over the slopes of the hills which surround the centre. As we neared the centre, I felt myself being engulfed in smoky, noisy, traffic-sodden concrete canyons. I don't know who said it is the most beautiful city in the world, but on first impressions I certainly did not agree. I must admit though, the city does boast a lot of palm trees and banyan trees (or something akin to them) which are an asset.

On the plane from London, I had been given the address of a university hostel, where it was possible to stay for nothing, so my first job in the city was to check that out, but unfortunately it was full up. No luck so far, but never mind, the day was young and what was there that I wanted to see in

Rio? Well I knew about the Corcovado, so that seemed a good place to start.

I found the number of the bus I needed, but like many large cities, it was a considerable time before I finally found someone who knew the place from which the bus departed, in the meantime having been given a lot of wrong directions I walked back and forth all over the place getting nowhere.

The bus took me to the bottom of the hill, from which a rack railway runs to the Corcovado at the top. The price (return fares only) of over £1 seemed extortionate, so I decided to walk up the road. I could see the statue of Christ just up on the hill, it didn't look very far away. I was soon to find that it was the enormous size of the statue which made it appear much nearer than it really was. I clambered up the steep road and had just begun to realise my mistake, when a car stopped and offered me a lift to the top for 10 cruzeiros (about 60 pence), so I accepted.

The statue, faced in a sort of uniform coloured mosaic, is truly enormous, being 40 metres high and weighing with its base, 1,200 tonnes. The view of Rio sprawled out beneath, the sea, the coastline, the hills and the Sugar Loaf in particular, is superb. From there, where you can hear no noise, see no traffic, no piles of uncollected rubbish, Rio does appear to be the most beautiful city in the world.

I walked back down the mountain enjoying the sight of blue azaleas, busy Lizzies, blue iris, banana trees, hibiscus and general jungle. Suddenly the strap broke on my rucksack, so I had to sit down at the side of the road and sew it back together again. Not a very good omen for my first day on the road I thought. The other strap had given way five years previously in New Zealand and even then the rucksack was old. Perhaps I should have retired it and launched out on another one for this trip, but it was too late to think about that now.

I returned to town and after a few more directional complications caught a bus to the National Museum. Wherever I go I always try to visit a represent-ative museum in each country, as I think it gives me an indication of the culture of that country and its historical foundation. I walked through a rather fine and impressive park and up to the even more impressive museum, which until 1889 had been the home of the Emperors of Brazil. The museum has an exceedingly comprehensive collection including what is probably its most famous item, the 'Bendego' meteorite. Found in Brazil in 1888 and weighing 5,360 kilogrammes it is the largest known metallic meteorite to fall on Earth.

Back in the centre I changed 20 dollars' worth of traveller's cheques at the bank, which I was later to learn was not advisable, as there are exchange houses which give a better rate. So I hadn't done too well money wise on the first day. It's difficult though until you know the ropes of an entirely new country, especially as I had not yet found any Brazilians who spoke English.

That evening as it was beginning to rain I tracked down the youth hostel and thankfully they accepted my very much out of date hostel card. Though at 30 cruzeiros per night (1 cruzeiro was equivalent to about 6 pence) I considered it an extortionately priced luxury.

As I lay in bed, tired, with sore feet, already a bit hungry, I listened to the thunderstorm outside and reflected on my first day in Brazil. I had wasted a bit of money and a lot of energy walking around the streets getting nowhere. Though that's not quite true, as I had seen a few miles of Rio in the process. Most of all though, I was beginning to find my feet, having subconsciously learned a lot more about Rio and Brazil, which as a traveller I needed to know. One thing I did know, was that I could not afford to stay in Rio, I should have to leave in the morning.

Feeling a little more confident and knowing my way around Rio a little better, I left the hostel the following morning and went to the market to study food prices. Food seemed to cost a lot, more than in England, but bananas were reasonably cheap. That's all right, you can live on bread and bananas — well, at least until something else turns up. So armed with a kilo of bananas, I went to the long-distance bus terminal and for 9 cruzeiros caught a bus to Petrópolis. That would get me clear of the city, for Petrópolis was the nearest town marked on my map on the road north.

In the hostel I had met a German youth, who I tapped for information. Among other things he told me that hitching was not possible in Brazil. I've heard that sort of talk before about many places, but I never believe it until I try it for myself. Besides, hitching had to be possible, because I could see that public transport was going to be prohibitively expensive.

The road climbed up out of Rio, through some very picturesque forested hill country, before descending into the surprisingly pleasant little city of Petrópolis. The reason for it being surprisingly pleasant, is because, as I later learned, it used to be the summer residence of the Emperor Don Pedro II. Consequently it became the fashionable place to spend the summer, for the rich of Rio de Janeiro.

On asking for the road north out of the city, I was directed every time back to the bus station. This continued to happen all the time I was in South America, even after I had learned how to say that I wanted to walk there. They could never understand that anyone should really want to walk and no doubt they considered they were doing me a favour by directing me to the bus station instead. After much pointing at my boots and suchlike gestures, I eventually found the road out of Petrópolis and ten minutes later along came my first lift.

He was a student going just a couple of miles further on to his home for lunch. He spoke one or two words of English and invited me back for something to eat. We arrived at an extremely palatial and luxurious house, where I was cordially greeted by his parents and entertained to a meal of potatoes, beans and rice. I was also given a detailed map of Brazil and the address of a relative in Brasilia. She apparently could speak English and would be able to help me when I arrived in the capital. In the afternoon I was driven back to the main road and feeling much happier and considerably more confident to face the continent, I continued walking north.

The road passed between jungle-covered mountains, but alongside the road was a conglomoration of colour washed concrete hovels, a mass of telephone and electric wires, scrap iron, old engines, tyres and battered cars. A few scraggy banana trees grew amongst the chaos, beneath which, in the rough grass or bare rubbish strewn earth, scrawny chickens scratched for survival.

After a few kilometres two youths picked me up. I was glad to be under cover, as soon after the rain came down in torrents. They drove, as everyone seems to in Brazil, at frightening speed and as we cornered I remember thinking, 'if we have a blow-out, it's curtains for the lot of us'. Suggestive thinking, for two minutes later we did, but thank goodness in a back tyre, while on a straight piece of road.

They drove 180 kilometres further on to Juiz de Fora, to an uncle's farm, where I spent a delightful evening being hospitably entertained by the family. How do you converse in a situation like that? Well it's not too easy, as only the aunt was able to speak just a few English words, but being notoriously bad at languages I have previously found myself in many similar situations. I have always found that a sense of humour is universal and along with a bit of international sign language, it is surprising how well you can overcome the communication barrier. One thing which did amuse my hosts enormously, was the English way of holding my knife and fork. They could not understand why anyone should use their fork upside down. They all tried, but without much success, the whole operation ending up in great hilarity.

As I lay in my sleeping bag on the floor and for the second night listened to the thunderstorm outside, I was beginning to wonder if it always rained. If it did, then that really was going to be a problem, especially at night-time, as I couldn't always expect to find shelter. Still if the hospitality offered to me on my first day's actual travelling in Brazil was anything to go by, things were not going to be so bad after all. I think by then the culture shock was over, I had accepted my position in the environment, learned the initial basic things about Brazil that were immediately essential, and was ready and waiting to face all that lay before me.

I was not ready and waiting in the morning though, when my host suddenly presented me with a pair of trousers as a souvenir. I was a bit surprised and didn't want them, but not wanting to offend, I accepted them all the same, thinking that maybe somewhere on the road I could pass them on to someone else, or swap them for a meal or a night's lodging. As things turned out, I ended up wearing them for my entire journey, until they finally fell to pieces right at the finish. I didn't like them and consequently never worried about what happened to them. They were too big and certainly didn't look very elegant. It is necessary to remain as clean and tidy as possible when travelling, but it is definitely not advisable to look smart and prosperous. There are far too many people on the road quite willing to lighten the load of the unwary traveller.

Breakfast consisted of bread, butter, cheese and instant coffee. That rather surprised me, as in a coffee-producing country like Brazil, I would have expected the real thing. But then few things are quite as we expect them to be.

Before the two lads drove me back to a suitable hitching spot on the road, my hostess gave me a card with their address on, in case I should get into trouble and need someone to turn to. That, I thought, was real hospitality and very comforting. What was not so comforting, though I am not quite sure what they meant by it, was that my hosts said that I must be crazy, courageous, or mad, to hitch in Brazil. Maybe I would find out in time, though I hoped not.

Throughout the day I obtained a number of lifts, travelling through hill country, some forested, but mainly cleared as grazing for cattle. In places I saw quite a large quantity of anthills, mainly about 60 centimetres high, though some must have reached a height of 1½ metres. In one field I was astonished to see a lot of brightly coloured lumps, some red, others blue, white, yellow and so on. I looked again and found that they too were anthills! Some colourful minded Brazilian had painted them.

At 4 in the afternoon I was dropped off on the outskirts of Belo Horizonte. The iron mining city, surrounded by a multitude of shanty homes is, in my opinion, a ghastly scar on the landscape. Most of the homes I passed that day were pitiful, some of them just open-ended thatched huts.

That near to the Equator it becomes dark about 6 o'clock, night and day being of equal duration. Just after dark I was dropped off at a road junction and toddled off to find a patch of grass to stretch my sleeping bag out on. A lorry driver had bought me some sandwiches during the day, so after a few of my bananas for an evening meal, I turned in for the night. Near by was a sentry style box, for what purpose I have no idea, but a retreat for me should it happen to rain. There often is not, but I feel much happier if there is some shelter handy.

Now was my chance to put to the test my home-designed mosquito net. In reality it was a large bag of mesh curtain, with elastic around the opening. The idea being that rucksack and boots were put in first, then when I am in my sleeping bag, I pull it over my top half, so that the elastic grips somewhere around my middle. Wearing my hat, which I invariably do anyway when sleeping out, the brim holds the net away from my face. The result, and highly effective I found it to be, was that no insect could sting me and no poisonous spider or snake could crawl into my sleeping bag, boots or rucksack. There was as I could see only one drawback. It was white, whereas all the rest of my equipment was of a good camouflage colour. When sleeping out I always try and tuck myself away, so that no one will know where I am.

Up at dawn, a few more bananas for breakfast and back on the road. Luck was with me, I hitched a lift in a lorry going all the way to Brasilia. Soon after we started I noticed a black insect the shape of a bee, but about 4 or 5 times the size, crawling up the windscreen. Suddenly the driver, a huge Negro, saw it, let out a yell and in panic chased it around the cab, quite forgetting that he was in charge of a lorry of considerable tonnage travelling at considerable speed. The result of all this being that the insect was splattered, as we could have been also, because in the turmoil we left the road in excess of 40 miles per hour, but luckily there didn't happen to be anything in the way. I asked the driver in sign language if the insect had a severe sting. He assured me with great gusto that it did.

The countryside had become much drier, now mostly scrubby bushland, which reminded me very much of parts of Kenya. Everywhere though there were anthills, some of them even up in the trees, which was a completely new sight to me. One type of tree, the Barrolandia, was particularly noticeable and continued to be prevalent for a further thousand kilometres or more. At that time of year it did not seem to have any leaves, but it did have the most beautiful primrose yellow clusters of flowers, which being located at a higher level than the surrounding bush, were visible for a mile or more.

During the course of the day, we also saw over a dozen bush fires raging, some we actually drove through. I suppose the country is so vast that no one takes any notice of them, for in time they burn themselves out, or keep burning until it rains.

I was dropped off at 8 p.m. in the centre of Brasilia, the new capital of Brazil since 1960. All I had bought on the entire trip so far since Rio, were two glasses of milk, so perhaps Brazil wasn't going to be too costly after all.

First I went in search of the relative of the people who had been hospitable to me in Petrópolis. She lived near the centre and on hearing of my recommendation, invited me in for a meal and a talk, being the first Brazilian I had met with whom I could hold a conversation. She phoned around to try and find me accommodation for the night, but without success.

Later in the evening I left and Brasilia being a spacious city, had no trouble in finding a large patch of unused and unlit ground near the centre, to sleep on. My hostess was under the impression that I was going in search of a hotel. I didn't want her to think otherwise and so make her feel awkward about not accommodating me.

I was up just as soon as it was light, as I didn't want to be found sleeping there. From what I knew, it was not a good idea to run foul of South American police.

After restocking with bananas I went for a potter around the city. It's vast, partly because there are so many open spaces, but that's the advantage of building a city from scratch and having practically unlimited land on which to do it. To one who dislikes modern architecture, it's not at all bad, in fact it's quite pleasant. It does not dwarf something old and historic, as might be the case in Europe. It does not pretend to be anything but what it is, ultra-modern. The beauty of the city is unique, in that it has been plannned as a city, not as collections of individual buildings which merge into the haphazard arrangement we usually have.

The cathedral, built in the shape of the crown of thorns, is certainly interesting. It appears miniature from the outside, but really the main area is underground. I walked down a ramp past statues of four saints, entering the circular nave which is all paved in white marble. Dotted around the floor are some cubes of similar marble to sit on. Most unusual, but charming in its modern simplicity.

Having walked around the city for three or four hours and seen what I wanted, I went into the post office to send a letter back to England. 5.20 cruzeiros. For that exhorbitant amount I could buy three days' supply of bananas.

Sightseeing and business completed, I walked to the central bus station, in order to take a bus to get clear of the city. There I met Joe, a black lad from Trinidad on his way home and going in the same direction as me. We caught the bus out of the city and then hitched north on the long road to Belém. By nightfall, after two lifts, we found ourselves only 70 kilometres further on at a roadside bar. After a meal of beans, rice and tomatoes, we waited around for a promised lift which never showed up. Not an uncommon occurrence in South America, as I frequently found out.

That night I shared a ditch with a litter of dead puppies, until it started to rain and I had to seek the shelter of the bar veranda. It rained all day and by evening we had only obtained one lift for 50 kilometres. That left us with a walk of 10 kilometres to the next bar where we could shelter from the rain. The bars or postes as they are called, are really garages, bars and restaurants, which are situated all along the roads in the remoter areas of Brazil. However, I was not to come across a similar convenience in other South American countries I was to visit. After our 10 kilometre walk in the dark, with night birds flying around us and the whirring sound of frogs in their thousands, we eventually groped our way into the poste. The owner greeted us, gave us a free meal and allowed us to sleep under his veranda.

In the morning after a free breakfast of bread and milk, Joe and I set to and cleared up the restaurant in return for the hospitality given us. As we worked a truck driver came in and promised us a lift for 1,000 kilometres, starting that evening. We were delighted and to pass the time, went down to the local river with some boys from the poste for a swim. The murky river flowed through thick overhanging jungle vegetation. Were there alligators in there? I couldn't help but wonder, though surely if the locals went swimming it must be all right, so I went in too. Had I known then what I was to see later, I should not have been so sure.

That evening our hopefully awaited truck driver turned up, along with a few friends to begin an orgy of feasting. Luckily they couldn't eat it all, so Joe and I finished it up for them, before lurching off into the dark to some unknown destination, on top of a swaying load of concrete pipes.

At some unearthly hour we arrived at the water purification plant of some out of the way one horse town. After an enforced tour of inspection, a lecture on water purification in Portuguese and numerous cans of beer, Joe and I slept somewhere in that maze of concrete corridors and tangle of pipes and valves.

In the cool light of dawn we lurched back on to the road again, Joe and I clinging grimly by our finger nails to that distinctly uncomfortable load of pipes. That morning we must have dropped altitude, for by midday we were travelling through an exceedingly hot dried up scrubby forest. Once we stopped for a rest in the shade of some trees and there the driver showed me a bush, not unlike a bramble, but when he flicked the leaves with his fingers, they quickly closed up. The driver could not tell me the name of the bush. So often I was to see fascinating or beautiful plants, but very rarely could any one tell me what they were.

As we travelled on there was very little to see, except the odd rocks painted white by bored government workers. There were of course the numerous bars along the dusty pot-holed road. We stopped at most of these and as the lorry came to a halt, the driver would push his head out of the window, look up at us and with a wide grin on his face, come out with his one and only stock English phrase, 'A snake in the glass.' This was accompanied by roars of laughter and the international hand sign meaning we are stopping for a beer. At one bar we took on board a buxom wench in a very tight fitting mini mini skirt. A few miles further on we pulled off the road once more, amongst pot-holes and clouds of choking red dust. She was home and we were in yet another brothel, drinking yet another 'snake in the glass'.

The driver, rather fancying the prostitute he had picked up, unfortunately decided to stay the night. While he drank the afternoon away, I dozed on a pile of beer crates in the corner of the bar. Perched high up and out of the way, I watched gigantic spiders crawl over the bare mud walls and low, bulging, dusty ceiling of rotting sticks. Occasional puffs of wind blew through the holes which were the windows and doorway, stirring the dust and sand into a choking haze in that hot murky room. Through half-closed eyes I watched tough, burly, over-developed girls come and go. They wasted little energy on conversation, but grabbed bottles of beer, bit off the tops with their teeth, spat them out and downed the beer at a rate which would impress any hard drinking English male.

At two in the morning, Joe and I were wakened from our sanctuary of concrete pipes, by our driver who was obviously in a bad nervous state. Apparently as he lay in bed with his prostitute, a burly man had smashed his way into the room, pointed a revolver at him and claimed the girl for himself. Having warped senses of humour, Joe and I had the greatest difficulty in keeping a straight face in front of our distressed driver. Unsuppressed laughter echoed out of our respective concrete pipes, only to be drowned by the noise of the accelerating engine as we lurched off into the night.

Three days and many lifts later we eventually arrived at Belém. The further north we went the hotter and more humid it became. The dust from the road stuck to our damp clothes and became red mud. Dust choked our mouths and nostrils and stuck to our perspiring faces, drying and cracking in the heat of the sun. The vegetation became greener, in parts thickly forested. Clearings had been made in the jungle. In these there were banana plantations, paddy-fields and herds of brahmin cattle. Along that dusty or muddy road, depending on the frequent downpours of rain, overhung by tall forest trees stretching for the light, fluttered myriads of birds in bright plumage. Many of the people began to look distinctly Indian, with their straight black hair and Mongoloid features. With a twinge of excitement I felt that at last we were nearing the great Amazon river, with all its animals, insects, Indians and strange fascination.

Perhaps I have over-simplified the difficulties of hitching the 3,000 odd kilometres from Rio, to Belém at the mouth of the Amazon. There seem to be three distinct groups of people who use the highway. Firstly there are the rich landowners, who in wide-brimmed straw hats and moustaches, speed from ranch to ranch, or ranch to bar in open Chevrolet pick-up trucks. Secondly, there are the poor people who go about their work in delapidated two-wheeled horse-drawn carts. Thirdly, there are the lorry drivers, the only ones who might possibly give you a lift. Even then it's practically impossible to hitch a lift on the open road. The only way is to wait at a poste or police check-point and talk with the driver, though even that's not easy without a common language. Drivers are suspicious of being attacked by bandits, so invariably they carry a knife, truncheon or revolver in the cab. Having persuaded one driver of our non-malevolent aims, he pleaded with us to accompany him, when he branched off west at Pôrto Franco to follow the Trans-Amazonica Highway. He offered to feed us and even pay for lodgings *en route*. He did however find someone else at the crossroads bar willing to go with him, so we continued our journey north. It appeared that the driver wanted security of numbers, because he was afraid of being ambushed by Indians on that long lonely road, apparently a very real danger.

Ten days after leaving Rio, I arrived at night in the city of Belém, grimy, suffering from the onset of dysentery, but now quite at one with this new continent. England now seemed unreal, this was the real world. Joe and I pottered off around the city and soon found an open-sided classroom, on a traffic island of all places. We tucked ourselves away behind some desks and laid our sleeping bags out on the floor. I lay down in the sanctuary of darkness, looking out on the bustling city and reflecting on the first leg of my journey. I had spent less in all that time and over 3,000 kilometres, than I had spent in one day in Rio.

CHAPTER 2

AMAZONAS

Joe and I found that the official passenger ship to Manáus did not leave for a further ten days. We sneaked through a warehouse and past the guards into the docks and did the rounds of all the boats and ships, trying to find one going to Manáus, but without success. Well not quite all the ships, for while I was scooping up handfuls of shelled Brazil-nuts which had been spilt on the quay, a guard spotted us and threw us out of the docks.

Not to be outdone, we then went to the military airport, to see about hitching a lift on a plane. One pilot promised us a lift the next day, but told us that we must first obtain offical permission from headquarters.

We tried to converse politely with the guard at the gate, but although we had been earlier assured that headquarters would be open, he was adamant that they were closed that day. Besides, I wouldn't be allowed in because my shirt was dirty. What an attitude! Just because I hadn't washed it since England, but I couldn't help that, I hadn't had a chance. I muttered something to the guard that 75% of Brazilians would be automatically barred from official government buildings, but that comment I feel was not appreciated. Clean smart clothes seem to be synonymous with civilisation to the majority of Brazilians. As long as a man is dressed smartly he is civilised. The fact that he continually spits all over the place and urinates in the street is immaterial. Having set up home on the floor of the military airport departure lounge (living on bread, water and my half rucksack full of acquired Brazil-nuts), we set out again the next day for military headquarters, me toeing the line by wearing a newly-washed though still wet shirt. It was no good. We were foreigners and consequently not allowed on Brazil's military planes.

Having made ourselves at home in the airport though, we still continued to use it as a base for three more days, while we combed the waterfronts for a way of travelling upstream. We found some small cargo boats going our way, but the captains could not be bothered to fill in reams of complicated official papers. These were apparently required by law before they could take us aboard.

The waterfronts were busy, noisy, colourful, fascinating and a shambles. Little sailing fishing boats tied up, bustling with activity, unloading an impressive variety of strange looking fish on the quay. An incredible collection of small live fish swam around in polythene-lined baskets, destined no doubt for the tropical fish tanks of North America and Europe.

I wandered amongst the rickety market stalls, past piles of oranges, bananas, coconuts, pineapples and tamarisk. Past clumps of rotting fruit and vegetables, to where primitive witch doctor medicines were being sold alongside Christian crosses. Pickled snakes in bottles, dried boa constrictors' heads, cow's horns, horse's hoofs, preserved lizards and a host of things I couldn't recognise.

Eventually we found a captain who would take us as far as Santarém, about half-way to Manáus. Before we boarded the 25 metre cargo boat *Fe em Deus* (Trust in God), we bought ourselves a couple of cheap hammocks in a closing down sale. We had been warned that they were necessary, as it was not feasible to sleep on the floor. During the daily tropical storms the decks would be flooded. On boarding the boat we found that it was already packed full and that rows of hammocks were strung up under the open-sided canopy which covered the deck.

On the first day we steamed through a maze of narrow channels between islands. There was no way one could tell where or how wide the actual river was, or even if we were part of it at all. I lay in my hammock or leant over the rails all day, fascinated at the panorama which unfolded before my eyes. Everywhere thick verdant jungle crowded down to the water's edge, spilling over into the brown murky river.

Occasionally we passed little wooden shacks on stilts by the water's edge. Washing hung limp in the humid mosquito-infested stillness. Often brown naked children played on the crude jetties, where small boats or dugout canoes were tied up. A German missionary on his way back to worldly obscurity, saw me watching the children and came over to talk. He told me that 40% of Brazilians are illiterate, though the government only admits to a figure of 10%. The other 30% can only write their names. Although school is supposed to be compulsory in many areas, there just are none. At that time to register a new-born child, it cost 200 cruzeiros (about £10) which a lot of people do not have. But if a child is not registered, then that child is not allowed to go to school.

As the channels became wider we passed some sawmills, where rafts of logs were tied up to overhanging trees. Little tugs chugged downstream to the mills, pulling immense rafts of logs behind them.

Then we turned down a dark gloomy channel through a tunnel of overshadowing trees, although the distance from bank to bank must have been at least 100 metres. This channel connected us with the main stream of the Amazon, and for the first time I could see the true magnificence of this the mightiest of rivers. It is difficult to judge distance over water, but I felt that the river must have been at least 5 kilometres wide at that point. We kept close to the bank as we steamed upstream. By doing this we kept out of the main, fast flowing current. Frequently gaunt dead trees with branches spiralling heavenwards, swirled past. Great clumps of water-lilies drifted by on their way to the Atlantic ocean. The Amazon is the greatest profusion of the living and the dead. Everywhere is life and everywhere is the result of life, decay.

I imagine that beneath the murky surface of the water lie more harsh realities of life and death. While watching out for alligators on the banks, or musing on the aquatic life, I saw many huge carp-like fish leap from the water. They were about 2 metres in length. A cold shiver ran down my spine when I saw their rows of needle sharp teeth. A Brazilian on board, noticing my interest, told me that the previous year a boat had sunk near Manáus with 200 people on board. Only 30 reached the shore, the rest were devoured by those monstrous man-eaters.

As we journeyed upstream we stopped off at many shanty villages to unload our cargo of beer, a very necessary luxury in that steaming humid heat. In fact I was quite surprised at the number of villages we saw. True they were usually a collection of only half a dozen or so home-built wooden huts on stilts, with thatched or shingle roofs, but it was habitation nevertheless. Occasionally there were small farms on the river bank, where the jungle had been cleared to grow sugar cane, or to keep cattle.

On the third day since Belém we arrived at the town of Santarém, a particularly unattractive but utilitarian town of box-like concrete buildings. We were in luck! There was a boat just about to leave for Manáus with a cargo of oranges. Joe battled for space to string up our hammocks, while I just had time to dash into town to buy a large bunch of bananas.

For four more days we steamed against the current in that smaller, dirtier, smellier and noisier boat. Every afternoon it rained, but on the first day out of Santarém, we had a tropical thunderstorm the like of which I have never seen before. I lay in my hammock clear of the rain-lashed deck, occupying the afternoon by cutting my hair, then with the aid of a squid of damp tobacco and a knife, prising out lice from under my skin.

Food on board the boats was limited invariably to rice, beans and coffee. It may seem dreadfully monotonous to Europeans, but as far as I could see, most Brazilians only ever eat rice and beans and maybe a little meat for every meal. One day we were surprised to find a change of menu, cold spaghetti. I grinned at two Italian missionaries who were on board and pointed to the bowl, but they only groaned and returned to their sole diet of bananas and oranges.

Drinking water was available from a tank on deck and foolishly I drank from it like everyone else. It was some days before I realised that it was water just taken straight from the Amazon. From then on I only drank it from my water bottle, with chlorine tasting purification tablets added. But in the meantime it had served to increase my dysentery.

At dawn we arrived at the decaying rubber boom city of Manáus. It was my intention to travel on up the Amazon into Peru, so I immediately began combing the waterfront for another boat going upstream. There wasn't one, but I was assured, "There may be one tomorrow, or next week, or it may be the week after that, but there will be one." *Mañana*, I was quickly learning, was the South American's universal answer to when anything will happen. They only tell you that, because they think that is what you want to hear, but tomorrow never comes. Doubt was beginning to enter my mind. Once I left Manáus, there was no way out by road for over 3,000 kilometres. The further upstream I went, the smaller would be the settlements and the less frequent would be the river traffic. I could end up stuck in the middle of nowhere for months and I couldn't afford the time or money. So I comforted myself with the thought that I had seen enough of the river and decided to hitch south-west on the Trans-Amazonica Highway into Peru instead.

Joe was hitching north to Venezuela and so back to Trinidad. Now was the time to say goodbye. We had travelled together since Brasilia, had helped each other and been company, but even so I was glad once more to be on my own, free and master of my own fate.

Before boarding the raft or 'balsa', to cross to the south side of the Amazon, I was accosted by a customs officer who demanded that I should fill in a declaration form. I couldn't even read it let alone fill it in, so the exasperated official just looked in my rucksack and let me go. The crossing, which took 45 minutes, is downstream from where the river Negro and Amazon join. It was fascinating to see how the two rivers flowed side by side, a knife edge distinction between the murky brown waters of the Negro and the clean Amazon.

I hitched for several hours beside the dirt road, before a van gave me a lift for 100 kilometres deep into the jungle. The road was still in the process of being made and *en route* we had to board three ferries. Two because new bridges had collapsed and one because no bridge had yet been built. Also once where the road had subsided into the swamp, we had to make a diversion through the jungle over tree trunks laid side by side.

At dusk we arrived at a rough pioneer style town in the making. Crude huts built on balsa rafts floated on the river. A few simple shanty thatched huts clustered along the muddy pot-holed road. All of it, even the foliage by the road, the rough hard drinking Brazilians and the empty beer cans strewn everywhere, all covered in red dust turned to mud.

Beyond all this were swamps. Forests of dead white trees stretching out of their reflections, shining in the still black waters. Dragon-flies skimmed over the surface. Alligators moved, barely discernible, hardly leaving a ripple behind them. Beautiful white stork-like birds stood around the swamp, while unseen birds in the jungle called out, their echoing voices accentuating the still empty silence.

After dark I crept into the shadows of a half-built petrol station, but by six the next morning, I was back on the road again. It was midday before the first lorry came by, but despite my frantic hitching it went on past, leaving a long trail of choking red dust behind it.

Brazil – an Amazonian village

Brazil – Jungle swamp 100 miles SW of Manáus

With no one to talk to and unknown hours to wait, one's mind can become over-active. Insignificant problems can blow up out of all proportion, giving concern for one's sanity. So as not to become my own worst enemy, I was often to find a need to empty my mind, go into a sort of mental trance, to learn infinite patience in that land of *mañana*.

Endless patience wasn't needed that day though, for a few hours later a second lorry came along and this time it stopped. Many female arms reached down over the boarded side of the open truck and hoisted me aboard. A double bed stood resplendent amongst crates of beer. Six girls bulging out of the clothes of their trade looked me over, then moved up making room for me to sit on the bed. My amusement at finding myself in the bizarre situation of travelling through Amazonas with a load of prostitutes moving house, was soon to take on a new light. The girls were laughing and joking, biting the caps off the beer bottles and continually swigging as an antidote to the heat. Suddenly there was silence. One girl cowered in the corner frightened. The other girls pounced on her, knocked her teeth out, then screaming and sobbing she was thrown out of the lorry, with all her belongings strewn out along the road after her. I was a little stunned by this sobering experience but as the girls then explained to me, she was seen stealing one of the other girl's flick knives, so she only got what she deserved. That's the law of the jungle I suppose! Despite the independence and ferocity of those girls, I found them to be shy, though friendly and generous. Whenever we stopped to eat, they would light a fire by the roadside, cook up rice, beans and coffee and insist that I shared in their meal. But I couldn't help looking at their five smiling faces and thinking of the other one, covered in blood, toothless, abandoned and seemingly forgotten.

All night the lorry clattered along the narrow, rutted but arrow straight road, stopping only at river crossings, where we were transported across by raft. Lying on the bed, peering out from under a tarpaulin which covered us from the cold of the night, the passing jungle seemed endless and awfully still, though not quiet, for there were constant shrill chatterings from unseen insects and birds.

That lift and unforgettable experience came to an end the next morning at Pôrto Velho. After stocking up my rucksack with the cheap staple diet of bread and bananas, I looked at my map and asked which was the road out of town, heading west into Peru. Fortunately, for once I found someone who knew what I wanted. The road, I was told, which was plainly shown on the map, had not yet been carved out of the jungle. Instead I had no alternative but to take the only other road, the one going south through Mato Grosso for well over 2,000 kilometres. From there I could, I hoped, travel through Bolivia and so into Peru, a diversion of about 5,000 kilometres.

I walked out of town, even that was a feat of endurance, for the heat was intense, far worse than around the Amazon. The sweat poured off me as I stopped at every bit of shade to rest, cursing the weight of my rucksack. No sooner had I left the town than the road disappeared into miles of detours. Several hours later and after much walking along muddy tracks and many lifts in road construction workers' trucks, it was back to the so-called main road.

Settlers were building shanty huts alongside the road. Heaps of tree trunks smouldered as the pioneers strove to clear patches of virgin jungle for cultivation. Tough grimy men hung around makeshift thatched wooden bars.

When a lorry passed (I saw no private cars that day), it was impossible to see the other side of the road. I began to feel quite ill from the dust in my lungs, although I wore a wet handkerchief around my face. Sweat and dust made me filthy, not that I minded, for a layer of mud helps to keep the mosquitoes off. But people are not so keen to give you a life, though everyone was grimy, so perhaps it didn't make any difference. At midnight I was dropped off at a roadside bar and slung my hammock up for the night under a lean-to.

The following morning I considered myself very fortunate indeed when I was given a lift in the back of a cattle truck. A lot of other people were picked up as well, but when they were dropped off at their various destinations, I noticed that they paid the driver considerable sums of money. This was not so funny. Obviously I would be expected to pay and the fare would not be cheap. So when we stopped at a village and the two drivers went into a bar for a drink, I nipped up to the other end of the village and waited until they had left. Plenty of people stopped for me, but they all wanted money. So it was with the greatest difficulty that I eventually managed to get a free lift as far as the town of Rondônia. It seems as if that is one of the places where everyone asks for lifts and pays, due no doubt to the non-existence of public transport. I was rather concerned about this, as I had only travelled 400 kilometres from Pôrto Velho. By my map, I had over 2,000 kilometres still to go in Brazil, along similar isolated roads. There was no way I could afford to pay for lifts over that distance.

For hours I hitched in the funace-like heat of the day, with the sinking feeling that I was getting absolutely nowhere. In the evening I walked to a poste in town, where eventually a man who spoke a little English saw the manager on my behalf. The manager in turn told the petrol pump attendant to ask for a lift for me. Success was soon mine when two men in a giant of a timber lorry agreed to take me on board. I set off in high spirits for a journey of unknown destiny. Also 50 cruzeiros better off, thanks to a generous and sympathetic passing motorist who insisted on my taking it, to my embarrassment but gratitude.

At midnight the lorry shuddered to a halt outside a tiled, wood and mud shack, overshadowed by the oppressive ever-present jungle. I was quietly but cordially welcomed by the driver's relations, into the small two roomed house. The door was of rough hewn planks, no lock. No glass in the windows, just shutters. A picture of Jesus hung on the crumbling whitewashed walls. Some sleepy chicken, disturbed by the visitors, scratched at the dusty earth floor beneath the hand-made table and benches, which were the only furniture in the room. In the corner were two lorry tyres, along with a few sacks of beans and some hand agricultural implements.

Husband and wife, and the two children who shyly watched me from beyond the light of the oil lamp had, I imagined, originated from the Indian subcontinent. There seems to be quite a strong Indian influence in Brazil. But then Brazilians are generally a chocolate-coloured hodgepodge of humanity. I found no feeling of colour discrimination. I think that if there was much prejudice in Brazil, I would have noticed it when travelling with black Joe from Trinidad.

As the driver cooked us a meal of rice, beans and tomato over a primus stove, I tried to make friends with the shy children. These people were poor but generous, happy and civilized. Poverty can be picturesque or squalid, depending on the outlook of the poor. However poor you are, leaving your litter just anywhere, just throwing rubbish out of the window does not show poverty of pocket, but poverty of mind. There was so much unnecessary squalor to be seen in that house. Feeling perfectly at home and at peace with the world, I slung my hammock under the lorry for the remainder of the night.

The driver appeared in no hurry to continue his journey, for we hung around the house playing football and fishing with the children until the following evening. Endless patience was needed as I had no idea how long we were going to stay, for all I knew it could have been days, so in the afternoon I set my compass and disappeared for a quick jaunt into the jungle. I scrambled over dead trees, moss and a mass of verdant growth. Trees towered above me in the dank dark green gloom, the canopy of foliage far above letting through just a few rays of sunlight. Massive creepers hung in all directions, trailing tendrils. In my imagination every tendril looked like a green snake hanging limp, waiting. Ghostly bird calls echoed in the timeless distance, while gargantuan hairy spiders faded into the camouflage of barely penetrable flora with frightening ease.

We left that jungle oasis of hospitality in the cool of the evening, only to stop again at midnight for a few hours' sleep on top of the load. At midday when the driver and his mate stopped at the roadside for a cook up, I waded into a nearby river to wash my trousers, in situ, much to the bewilderment and amusement of some local women, who were doing their washing on the bank. They were not used to seeing men washing clothes and certainly not by a gringo in that strange fashion. The driver grinned as he handed me a bowl of beans and rice, also amused by this strange soggy foreigner who walked into rivers with all his clothes on.

For three more days the lorry crawled its way, often in first gear, south-wards along the monotonous pot-holed road. The driver weaved from side to side to avoid the worst of the ruts and holes, but it was the sand-filled ones which were the worst, you can't see those. We had just passed a lorry abandoned in the middle of the road, snapped completely in two by the unending stress of metal fatigue, when once more our wheels dug themselves into the quicksand. While we were grovelling under the lorry with spades trying to dig out a wheel, the driver suddenly, and with great excitement, pointed to the wall of vegetation which flanked the road. He had seen some Indians watching us from the jungle, but when I looked they had silently vanished. Feverishly we worked in silence, we were trapped and knew it. Green walls of jungle towered perpendicular from the edges of the narrow, rough, yellow, sandy road, which disappeared in both directions into perspective dots at infinity. We saw no more of those Indians, but it was with great relief when eventually our passport to freedom crawled its way clear of yet another sand pit.

Journeying southwards, the climate became blissfully cooler as the jungle gave way to rolling grassland dotted with scrubby bushes and stunted trees. Strange though, because for 300 kilometres I saw not a single cow or any form of cultivation, just the odd domed hut every now and again. We stopped by one of these huts, as the driver wanted to see what the occupant might have for sale. Lack of jungle to hide in has brought a certain degree of 'civilisation' to the Mato Grosso Indian, for the man who met us was dressed in rags which had once been a shirt and shorts.

His home was an impressively large dome, built of sticks lashed together, then thatched all over with leaves. We stooped down to enter by one of the two holes which were both doorways and windows. From the centre of the room a smouldering fire belched out smoke which filled the hut, then oozed out between the thatch, through which a thousand pin pricks of light vainly helped to illuminate the dim interior. Three young children played swings in one hammock, while mother unmoved by our presence lay naked in another, suckling her infant. Earthenware cooking pots and empty booze bottles lay scattered over the sandy floor. Against the woven wall was propped the Indian's bow and arrows, while alongside was a pile of deer skins, which the driver was earnestly inspecting with a view to buying.

A further day on the road and the open grassland began to give way to scrubby woodland. A landscape not out of place in England, except for the odd palm tree. Strangely, there were lots of what I can only assume were miniature coconut trees, complete with perfect nuts, though only the size of walnuts.

The population became denser and now men on horseback were in evidence, moving herds of brahmin cattle. Poste cafés became more numerous, which I thoroughly approved of, as we always seemed to stop at them for the free coffee which was usually provided. Some of the postes seemed quite neat and hygienic at a first glance, but the kitchens were invariably in a disgusting state to a European way of thinking, consequently leaving the 'estrangeiro' with constant diarrhoea.

After the city of Cuiabá (pronounced like the peculiar sheep), the now asphalt road wound through a range of thickly wooded hills. Palm trees were much in evidence and also many flowering pinheiro trees, covered in a most beautiful heather coloured blossom.

I began to sense that my lift was soon to end, for the driver and his mate started scrounging off me. They not only wanted me to buy their cigarettes — well fair enough, but they also wanted my knife, watch and everything else they realised I had. These I managed to hang on to, but with the mounting tension, the friendship we had made, quickly faded into a brittle battle of wits. Though when I was dropped off that afternoon at Rondonópolis, the driver very kindly asked a garage proprietor to try and fix me up with another lift.

Brazil — Indian hut, Mato Grosso

CHAPTER 3

BRIBERY AND CORRUPTION

While mending my broken sandals with old typewriter tape, found amongst the rubbish on the garage forecourt, a car pulled up for me. I was rather surprised, for not since my second day in Brazil had I been given a lift in a private car. The driver had, I assume, already driven a long way, he still had a long way to go and was in a hurry. I was quickly left in no doubt as to why I had been picked up. He wanted me to talk to him, non-stop, to keep him awake, not easy without a common language. By midnight, I too felt desperately tired, but as he drove like a bat out of hell and our safety was at stake, I somehow managed to keep up a constant conversation. Now and then as we tore down the dusty road, I prodded him, my hand hovering near the steering wheel as he nodded off to sleep.

At one in the morning, after what seemed an unnerving and endless night we eventually drove into Campo Grande. The driver, perhaps feeling that I had earned my lift, insisted on paying for a room in a hotel for me. It seemed like eternity since I had slept in a proper bed. Unadulterated luxury, marred only by the itching caused by bugs boring into my back.

The road west to Bolivia was apparently practically non existent, so after taking me out to breakfast, my driver took me to catch the daily train for the border town of Corumbá, over 400 kilometres west. But he was wrong about the departure time, so I missed it by half an hour.

With a frustrating 24 hours to wait, I set off to explore the city, replenish my food stocks, buy nails to repair my sandals and some hydrogen peroxide to alleviate a raging toothache. Asking for that in Portuguese was far beyond me, but the chemical symbols I wrote down for the chemist were international, the only practical use a study of school chemistry has so far ever been to me.

As I sat in the park sewing up my rucksack with fishing line, a man came and talked to me in English. Amazed and delighted I swamped him with questions, seeking information on all sorts of topics, for he was only the second Brazilian I had met who spoke English. A lack of spoken English seemed distinctly odd, when all over Brazil I had seen people in shirts bearing slogans written in English. North American imports I suppose, though there must be some British influence, for I was amused to see one which bore the legend, 'British beer is best'.

Our conversation led to an offer of a bed for the night. He would, he told me, meet me at the bus station at 8 o'clock that evening and take me back to the hotel where he was staying. I was rather cautious of his intentions, but went along at the appointed time, though rather surprised to find him there at all. With much whispering and peering around corners, I was eventually smuggled into his room. Once there behind locked doors, I had a bed to sleep in, while he and his wife slept in another. A similar undercover operation to smuggle me out at dawn, then after much gratitude on my part, off to catch the train on its twelve hour journey to Corumbá.

I was led to believe that second class was not to be recommended, not that that would make any difference to me, but I was pleasantly surprised to find upholstered seats and ample room. Not a case of having to fight for a luggage rack to sit on, as had so often been my fate in Asia. The carriages were obviously of pre-war construction, North American I should imagine, with rather quaint reversible backs to the seats, so allowing you to choose in which direction you wish to sit. Quite a luxury for 26 cruzeiros, as long as one is impervious to the ever-present and predominant stench of urine.

We rattled our way through pleasantly wooded country, past some forested sheer walled plateaux, reminiscent of *The Lost World*. Sir Arthur Conan Doyle must surely have known that those massive blocks and cliffs of sandstone, rising perpendicular from the plain, exist. Here in that thinly inhabited region, on those weird inaccessible forested plateaux, what strange life could indeed remain or have evolved?

Arriving at Corumbá on a Friday evening, I was horrified to find that Sunday and Tuesday's trains were fully booked. I had no choice but to kick my heels in the town until the following Wednesday. When I am travelling I don't like to stop just to idle, it's an expense of time, money and patience. But patience is a very necessary commodity in South America, the land of *mañana*. I found a reasonably cheap room in a back street. Not my usual procedure, but worth it if you are paying for 24 hours, not just a night, as then you have a base to rest, wash and mend clothes and leave a rucksack.

Corumbá with its colour washed concrete buildings and paved streets, was not an unpleasant place to spend a few days. Granted there was a certain amount of rubbish in the streets and the odd spotted pig running about, but generally it's a remarkably clean town. Maybe it is more wealthy than most Brazilian towns, for it is situated near the world's largest deposit of manganese. Nevertheless, the busy streets still had their fair share of delapidated horse-drawn taxis and exhausted vintage cars from the 1920-30s. The climate, though not the roads, must be conducive to minimal decay in motor vehicles. The owners obviously are not, as they seem to take no pride in their ancient machines.

Many of the people, well dressed in the main, wore ponchos. Corumbá is a border town, but I was rather surprised to see this influence from Bolivia. Few Brazilians travel outside their own country, because if they do, they are compelled to deposit a sum of money with the government, interest free for one year. At that time, the amount was equivalent to about £500.

My first job in the town was to report to the police station for my passport to be stamped. That was in lieu of immigration control and necessary before a train ticket would be issued to me. Police in Brazil seem to wield a great deal of power, which can be distinctly unnerving, as I was soon to find out. While I was in town innocently minding my own business, a policeman beckoned me to follow him back to the station. My passport was taken from me and using this, a typist filled in a form which was then handed to me to read. A month previously when I had arrived in Rio, I spoke not a word of Portuguese, but now I had learned enough to know that this form made me the owner of a car. Five policemen stood around me in that room and explained very carefully and patiently what I was to do. A Bolivian and his wife had a car (a policeman nodded to a rather scared young man in the corner of the room) which they wished to take back into Bolivia. However, for some reason the man had no passport, besides, to take a car into Bolivia involved paying enormous import duties. I, being a foreigner, would not have to pay any duty, so the car had been put into my name and I was to drive it across the border. That all seemed very straightforward to the police, who already knew from when my passport was stamped, that I was bound for Bolivia. But I was not so sure. Yes, I felt sorry for that Bolivian and his wife who obviously had problems, but I didn't and never could know all the implications behind it and had no wish to see the inside of a Bolivian gaol. That left me with a problem. I could say, "Yes I know what you want me to do, but I am not going to," which could have led to a nasty situation, as the police seemed to be all-powerful and distinctly corrupt. What I actually did was to appear to want to help, but pretended that I hadn't a clue what they were talking about. This charade was followed by telephone calls to various schools in the town, to find an English teacher who could translate, though without success. It was with some relief three hours later, when the police had come to the happy conclusion that I was a total idiot and probably incapable of driving a car anyway, that I was eventually released.

The train stopped at the border post, where we all dutifully left the train and passed through the squalid but seemingly effective customs shed. Well they checked my rucksack pretty thoroughly anyway. We had only just returned to our seats and still very much in view of the customs post, when a number of men stealthily approached the train, from the cover of trees on the opposite side of the track. Suddenly I was showered with parcels which were hurriedly pushed through a small window above my head. Eager hands grabbed them, silently but at lightning speed, dispersing them throughout the carriage. Even a dear old lady, who looked as if butter would not melt in her mouth, suddenly sprang into action. With a knowing wink at me she tucked away numerous packages under her voluminous skirts, appearing from then on to be considerably taller than she really was.

A girl sitting behind me leaned forward and to my surprise spoke to me in English. "Don't touch any of those parcels. Everyone in the carriage except you and I are smuggling. They have all bribed the customs men, but if we handle those parcels, we shall be in gaol." Mary, on her way home to La Paz, was incidentally the only Bolivian I was to meet who spoke any English. She went on to explain to me that most of what was being smuggled was fabrics. Bolivia has no factories, so consequently everything manufactured has to be imported, with a high duty to be paid.

The train rattled on through scraggy forest and swamplands. Once more I saw massive cliffs of sandstone rising sheer from the forest, plateaux even more awe-inspiring than before. Surely this forest would be ideal for clearance and cultivation, so why was it apparently practically uninhabited? Mosquito-infested swamps, Mary told me. No place for man to live, so consequently the road into Bolivia is nothing but a hazardous track. Hence the reason for my travelling by rail. Now aware of the problem, I noticed insects being blown in through the open window. As I shut it, the glass fell out, much to the amusement of all.

Later we did stop at a few villages *en route*, collections of wooden or mud brick homes roofed with thatch or red tiles. Boys converged on the train in hordes, desperately trying to sell oranges, cakes, chickens and fish. Cows wandered aimlessly across the track, while pigs foraged underneath the carriages. Hence the necessity of an old pioneer style cow catcher on the front of the train. To my knowledge, the mangled carcasses of at least one dog, two pigs and a calf were swept off the line that day.

Besides meeting Mary, who gave me her telephone number in La Paz in case I should need help, I also met on the train a Brazilian of roughly the same age as myself. Michello had come from Rio de Janeiro, six days by train, and was on his way to Peru to buy silverware, snake, jaguar and alpaca skins. These he was intending to smuggle back to Brazil, assuring me that he could make 1,000% profit on them.

Michello and I found a room to share that night in the back streets of Santa Cruz. Next morning after a breakfast of bread and milk, he went off to buy snake skins, while I went to change money and view the city. Unlike Brazil, the fixed bank exchange rate was realistic, so it was not possible to change money at a higher rate by some undercover or devious means (£1 equivalent to 30 pesos).

I found the city, in spite of its roofed over pavements, to be rather drab and uninspiring. Probably due to the fact that the once isolated city had doubled its sprawling population in the previous ten years to over 130,000, the result of exploitation of oil in the area. In the centre, as is the case in the vast majority of South American cities and towns, is the plaza, a little park with seats. Always a handy place for travellers. Adjoining the plaza, across a road of hexagonal interlocking cement blocks, is the weathered red brick colonial cathedral. Rather plain inside for a Catholic church, though possessing a wealth of hand-wrought silver, including a richly embossed altar front.

Late in the afternoon Michello and I set off to catch the daily bus to Cochabamba, but as there are half a dozen or more bus stations, we had considerable difficulty finding the right one. When we did, it had a striking resemblance to a war blitzed lavatory, so it's not surprising it was hard to find.

The bus wound its way through wooded hill country, fire-flies flashing against silhouetted mountains. We stopped at some little towns on the way, just a few simple tiled adobe brick houses bordering the wide, rough, earth road. People solemnly sat is if waiting for *mañana*, regardless of the hour or crisp coolness of the night. A few people lounged in the doorways of bars, silhouetted by the light of paraffin lanterns. The eerie silence was occasionally broken by a dog, somewhere, barking into the still night. No longer were we in the warm, verdant, tropical regions, but entering a new experience of bleak austere altitude, a contrast of climate and culture. Wooded hills gave way to mountains covered in coarse grass, with the occasional small adobe brick homestead scratching a bare existence from the stony ground.

Just as the sun rose into the cold, steel-blue sky, from behind snow-capped peaks, the bus rumbled through a jumble of single storey mud houses into the waking city of Cochabamba. The streets were already alive with local Indian women, streaming into the city to begin another day of haggling in the busy outdoor market. Dressed in colourful shawls and full skirts over multitudinous petticoats, the women trudged purposefully towards the market, with vivid rainbow coloured blankets on their backs, bulging with babies, fruit, vegetables and cloth. With their long, jet black, plaited hair protruding from beneath trilby or mini-sized bowler hats, they are totally uninfluenced by European fashion.

Many of the indigenous men have discarded their ponchos for often drab and tatty conventional clothing, except for their insistence on wearing colourful knitted caps with ear flaps. The bone structure of their brown leathery faces has a similarity to those of North American Indians or Eskimos.

Over the years the colonists of Brazil have intermarried with the native population, ending up with a hodgepodge of coffee-coloured inhabitants. Upon entering Bolivia, I was instantly aware that the same system did not apply. The minority of the population, those of Spanish stock, are European in dress, manners and racial descent. Consequently the vast majority of the inhabitants, especially in rural areas, retain direct ancestry back to the Incas or contemporary races.

The daily bus from La Paz did not leave until the evening, which was a great shame as I loathe to travel across land by night, so missing the scenery, even if it does solve the problem of somewhere to sleep.

I hadn't been in Bolivia long, but it was already patently obvious to me that hitching was totally out of the question. Bolivia must be pretty unique in just not having private motorised transport. Oh yes, there were some open trucks and lorries, but lifts were, as I was to find to my cost, unimaginably uncomfortable and always had to be paid for.

The bus was incredibly crowded, so there was no hope of sleeping. Even the gangway was full of Indians perched on piles of blankets, bundles and hessian sacks, which moved ominously as their live occupants fought for breathing space. Where there was one uncluttered stretch of gangway, women openly squatted, their urine flowing across the floor, soaking into bundles of clothing.

The bus clattered its way further and further up into the mountains along narrow, rough, boulder-strewn roads. I noticed that even the normally rowdy Indians went very quiet when we met a lorry and had to back down around a steep hairpin bend, with a perpendicular drop of hundreds of metres on one side. Dust from the road penetrated the bus, leaving a coating of grime on everything and despite a cloth around my face, left me feeling positively sick, as it ground its way into my eyes, mouth and lungs.

Crawling on to the edge of the Altiplano, the bus then sped across that vast flat plain of bare stony earth. Here and there we passed a few mud houses beside patches of ploughed land. Feeling stiff and bitterly cold, we were thankful when at last dawn came and the rising sun shone across the vast snow-covered plain, melting the frozen condensation from the windows of the bus. The road led to the edge of the Altiplano, then suddenly, without any warning, there far beneath us, cradled in a vast impressive basin between the mountains, lay the city of La Paz.

The centre of the city is quite European in design, but behind the seat of government, up the sides of the bowl, are a maze of fascinating streets and alleyways. From dawn to dusk those steep dirty cobbled streets are full of colour and noise, as crowds jostle and haggle. Fat old women in their bright skirts and bowler hats, sit outside mud brick houses selling piles of food and fabrics of all descriptions, amongst the chaos of tooting traffic jams.

There was so much I wanted to do and see in La Paz, collect my mail from the British Embassy, visit the Tiahuanaco museum, change money, seek out information regarding further transport and much more. It was a mistake. By rushing up and down those steep streets, I very soon found myself in a flea-ridden bed in a back street lodging house, with the most almighty headache — altitude sickness. For La Paz, the highest capital city in the world, stands at 3,600 metres above sea level.

At dawn the next day I said farewell to Michello and still nursing a frightful headache, set off to locate the bus for Tiahuanaco. Bus stops or stations seem to be non-existent, so it was some time before I eventually found the bus tucked away down a back alley. As the bus rattled its way out of La Paz we passed the military airport. Guards were building a snowman outside the main gate, while others from their watchtowers, were throwing snowballs down at passers-by.

Bolivia – Street market La Plaz

After an extremely bumpy ride for 70 kilometres across the Altiplano, we arrived at Tiahuanaco. The small peaceful Indian village, which is at a higher altitude than La Paz, is set on a flat plain under the shelter of mountains. Mud brick houses, tiled or thatched with grass, flank the mud or cobbled streets. But it wasn't the village with its old men squatting in the sun which I had come to see, rather the impressive ruins of great antiquity which lay near by. When the Spaniards first visited that bleak and lonely spot and saw the gigantic ruins, they asked the local Indians who had built them. But the Indians did not know, the memory of that civilisation had already been lost in the mists of time.

The ruins are fenced off, so together with two lads from the United States who I had met on the bus, I paid my admission fee. The ruins today are not what they used to be when the Spaniards arrived. The gigantic cut stones were joined together then with silver or copper tenons, which the invaders ripped out, toppling the stones. Now the temple, which seems to be the name given by the archaeologists to any building of unknown use, is being reconstructed. Unfortunately prior to this era, stones were removed for railway building and many fine statues were taken away to La Paz. In spite of everything, what is left is extremely impressive. Blocks of stone 100 tonnes or so each, geometrically shaped and fitted together to form mighty walls. The 'Gate of the Sun', 10 tonnes in weight, cut from a single piece of stone and decorated with unexplained carvings, is a remarkable piece of sculpture.

Finely carved but stylised statues stand sentinel over a desolate landscape. Why, when, how? The answers all remain an exciting but unexplained mystery.

Feeling weak and breathless from the exertion of clambering around the ancient site, the three of us headed back to the village, accosted *en route* by small boys selling 'genuine' statuettes from the ruins. It was only when I scratched through the grime on the base of one with my knife and pointed out to the lad that it was made of plaster, not stone, that we were finally left alone.

A sign by the side of a black hole in a mud brick wall, advertised the sale of tea made from coca leaves. Feeling that the cocaine extract might be just what we needed, we clambered down into the small dark dingy room of the one and only pension in the village and slumped over the rickety dusty table. The pale green tasteless tea had a practically magical effect. The altitude sickness left us and once more I felt glad to be alive.

After exchanging addresses with the two lads from the USA, John and Tony, who were living in Peru, studying Spanish, they left on the return bus to La Paz, while I bargained for a night's lodging at the pension. I knew that as soon as the sun set it was going to be bitterly cold on the Altiplano, so for 15 pesos a bit of shelter did not seem too extravagant. A girl led me through a door in a high wall which flanked a narrow alleyway. Beyond was a walled-in farmyard and opening on to this a simple mud brick room. Within, was a wooden chair and a bed covered in antiquated ponchos. On the crumbling wall was nailed a calender, many years out of date. The girl gave me a candle, then left, locking the yard door behind her, but promising to let me out at sunrise. I sat on the rickety chair outside my doorway in the farmyard, smoking my pipe and enjoying the evening. Then jamming a stick against the door to keep out the cold night air and unwanted guests, I turned in for the night.

The morning was warm, clear and exhilarating. Walking out across the Altiplano, quiet except for the birds singing, it reminded me of a perfect summer's day on the English moors. But there the likeness ended, for beyond the flat plain rose jagged snow-covered peaks. As I walked along the narrow rough country tracks I occasionally passed women, barefoot and dressed in traditional costume, driving donkeys laden with vegetables or firewood to the daily market in the village. As there were no hedges or fences, small boys herded pigs, sheep and cattle. Men trudged behind pairs of oxen, ploughing the open fields with antiquated wooden ploughs. By the scattered, thatched, mud brick homesteads, donkeys patiently waited, hobbled by their front legs. It's difficult to imagine that that peaceful but bleak plain was the original home of the common potato and the centre of the awe-inspiring and ancient Tiahuanaco civilisation.

On arriving back at La Paz, I just had time to buy a large bunch of bananas, before boarding another bus for the fabled silver mining town of Potosi. The bus shuddered to a halt somewhere on the Altiplano. It was pitch dark outside. The driver announced that we had trouble with the back wheel and that we would have to get off the bus while he jacked it up to fix it. For three hours I ran around the Altiplano, with my sleeping bag wrapped around me like a boa constrictor, trying to keep warm. It's no wonder the Incas and their ancestors worshipped the sun. The Altiplano has a beautiful climate by day, but by night it is one of the most inhospitable places man could wish to be. Where else does the sun have such a profound effect at dawn or dusk? Twice more during the night the wheel gave trouble, but after the first time, the passengers mutinied and refused to leave the bus.

As the sun rose, the iced over rivers thawed. Llamas grazed on the few tufts of coarse yellow grass which made a bid for existence among the stony soil. Others were penned in dry stone wall enclosures, attached to little grass thatched stone huts. The road snaked its way through the mountains, everywhere a backcloth of snowy peaks. I was not alone in being unnerved by the narrow, rocky, hairpin roads, winding their way around perpendicular cliffs. There was a general feeling of unease on the bus and a number of Bolivians were sick. The drivers are quick enough to use their horns in a traffic jam in the city, but they never thought it necessary to use them on those treacherous corners. If two vehicles met head on, I hate to think what the result would be. Little crosses on the side of the precipices and the twisted remains of vehicles thousands of feet below, don't help one's confidence either.

Potosi, at a height of 3,900 metres is the highest city in the world. It was also once the largest city in South America, for it was here in the sixteenth century that the Spaniards discovered the richest silver deposits ever known. Cerro Rico, the fabled silver mountain, now honeycombed with mine workings is four centuries later, still producing silver. But the international importance of Potosi has waned. Around the main plaza are some fabulous colonial houses dating from the seventeenth century, but beyond, sprawling up the hillsides, are the inevitable adobe huts of a scruffy mining town. There is an interesting variation in dress, in that the women wear traditional Welsh style hats rather that the universal bowler.

I walked out of the city, up into the rarefied atmosphere of the surrounding mountains. The wind moaned across the rocky slopes, flattening the coarse yellow grass over the wind weathered stones. Across the broad valleys sharp snowy peaks pierced the cold steel-blue sky.

No sooner had I arranged to rent a room in a pension for the night than the proprietor insisted, without explanation, that I follow him. I was taken to a military establishment and before I knew what was happening I was standing in the middle of a bleak stone room. As the door firmly closed behind me I found myself looking at a man in uniform seated behind a large desk. Pictures of wanted terrorists hung on the walls. He checked right through my passport, wrote down some notes and asked lots of questions. But as my Spanish was not tuned in for those kinds of questions, he didn't receive any sensible answers. He looked me up and down then wrinkled his

Bolivia – Cerro Rico, the silver mountain

nose. Yes I could smell my socks too, even with my boots done up tightly. They hadn't been off for 36 hours and washing socks was nigh impossible, as nothing dries in those sub-zero nights. After stamping my passport 'Interpol Visa', I was ushered off to 'Persons Identification' to be interrogated yet again before being released, though still none the wiser.

After my journey the previous day, I felt distinctly uneasy as I boarded the bus for Sucre. Both front tyres were as bald as a coot with large patches of canvas showing. As expected, he drove like a maniac along the precipitous roads and in one place where the road had disappeared, along a river bed.

It was interesting to notice that a lot of the women brush the road outside their houses, something that would not happen in Brazil. The women also spin wool as they go about their daily business, whether it's selling fruit in the market or ploughing with oxen in the fields.

At two in the afternoon, the bus arrived at the charming old colonial city of Sucre. I checked in at a pension and found myself sharing a room with a French Canadian lad. Together we wandered through the city admiring the fine old whitewashed buildings, in particular the beautiful seventeenth century cathedral and San Miguel, the oldest church in use in South America. We discussed our plans together, then decided to join forces and head west into 'the Andes. Marcello had heard of an interesting tribe of Indians who live in a remote area there. We thought it worth a visit.

At daybreak we boarded the bus for Oruro. As before the going was treacherous. On a number of hairpin bends the bus made three point turns, or if they were too steep, sharp and narrow, the driver reversed up alternate stretches between bends. I watched with horror through the back window as the rear of the bus overhung eternity on one bend. But still the driver carried on backing. Desperately I looked down at the ground a couple of thousand feet below, then frantically tried to work out how far along the bus the back wheels were. Still we went back, my nerve broke. Sweating and trembling I shouted to the driver. He stopped and the other occupants looked around at me twitching and laughing nervously.

On the outskirts of a village a man lay prostrate on the ground. I thought perhaps he was dead, but as we drew nearer to the centre of the village, the roadside was littered with them, obviously paralytically drunk. Around the square a festival was in full progress. Men in gay costumes were parading, carrying a cross, but by the amount of ear shattering explosives which were being thrown into the air and the seething mass of fighting bodies, to an onlooker the occasion seemed more pagan than Christian.

As Marcello and I booked into a cheap pension in Oruro, we were immediately whisked off to the police station for interrogation. I was beginning to think that this must be common form with foreigners.

At 5.30 in the morning we emerged on to the streets and into the sub-zero temperature of dawn. We had been told that presently there would be a truck which would take us west, out across the stony desert for at least part of our journey. Well of course there wasn't and we spent some very cold and uncomfortable hours, before finding out that one would be leaving at 2 p.m. We did eventually track down the elusive truck and at 3.30 p.m. to our great relief, it drove off. But no, we came back again. Four more times we drove around the city, loading up with people, their possessions, sacks of flour, crates of beer, cans of petrol and some sheeps' heads.

At 6.30 p.m. we did eventually begin our journey, with about forty Bolivians plus baggage and babies, in an open truck measuring no more than 2½ metres by 5 metres. Driving across the rough stony desert with the stars above and not even room to sit down or move, it was incredibly cold and uncomfortable. It would have been even colder if I hadn't 'borrowed' one of the driver's blankets. It smelt of stale urine, but that was of little consequence in those conditions.

At 8 o'clock in the morning we were dropped off 200 kilometres south-west of Oruro, numb with cold and cramp. But where were we? This was just the crossroads of two hardly discernible tracks across a desert, empty except for three or four adobe huts. We argued with the driver. He had told us he was going to the village of Sabaya, but now we were being dropped in the middle of nowhere. He had said he was leaving Oruro at two the previous afternoon, but had not left until four and a half hours later. They tell you what they think you want to hear, to keep you happy, but we were not amused at being left in the desert. At first we refused to pay, unless he carried out his promise by taking us to Sabaya, but eventually settled by giving him thirty pesos, instead of the seventy asked for.

Just as we started out in the direction the driver had pointed, an Indian came out of his hut and invited us home for breakfast. He directed us to leave our rucksacks inside his hut and then for us to sit outside in the sand. His wife gave us tea and bread, while he preoccupied himself with slaughtering a sheep in front of us and slitting it open. His son, I discovered later, was busy 'liberating' my tobacco from my rucksack.

Bolivia — Village street, Sabaya

CHAPTER 4

CAPTIVE IN THE DESERT

Sand-dunes and a dried up salt water lake seemed to stretch to infinity before us, or at least as far as the distant snow-capped peaks. Salt caked sand crunched beneath our boots and as the sun rose the glare from the white salt-encrusted desert became intense. The heat burnt into our skin, sapping our energy and melting the frozen rivulets which still meander across the bed of that vast salt pan. We stumbled on for thirty kilometres across that heat reflecting furnace, before arriving at a range of barren hills and the village of Sabaya which nestled beneath them.

It was uncanny, for there was not a soul in sight as we walked into the village along a dusty street, flanked by little thatched adobe huts. What would our reception be in this remote area? Would they be hostile? I hoped not, as somehow we had at least to obtain food there. My fears were in vain. Everyone seemed most friendly and within an hour we were installed in a classroom of the school, by permission of the governor. After the previous night it was blissful luxury to stretch out in our sleeping bags, on the plank floor between desks.

Being Sunday the next day school was closed, so we had the place to ourselves. The school was of mud, brick and thatched with grass. There was of course no electricity or heating, but there was a well in the sandy playground. Having once arranged to hire two bicycles for the following morning, the rest of the day was spent sewing clothes, washing them at the well and generally enjoying the chance of a rest.

In the evening I went to the bar to buy some bread and a couple of tins of tuna fish, in anticipation of the next stage of our journey. In the bar some Indians were drinking beer, playing musical instruments, singing and generally enjoying themselves. They demanded that I sit and drink with them, then gave me some rice and beans to eat. It was all very sociable but their generosity was embarrassing. They had had enough to drink, so I felt very relieved when eventually I managed to excuse myself. Drunks can turn nasty, especially when they expect you to buy a financially crippling round of drinks for everyone in the bar.

As the dawn shadows quickly shortened over the sand-dunes of the salt pan desert, we set our compasses and cycled out on to the still frozen salt-encrusted plain. As the sun rose fiercely into the clear sky, mountains appeared suspended in mid air, then vanished totally before our eyes. Before us lay a lake surrounded by luscious trees, shimmering in the reflecting glare of salt crystals. Then it too faded, our way then being blocked by sand-dunes towering high above us, but they were real enough. There was nothing imaginary about the sweat and labour in pushing our bikes over them. Llamas disdainfully looked up from the sparse clumps of bleached grass they were grazing on, stopped chewing and watched in what seemed like mild surprise and amusement as the two gringos struggled past.

With our boots slung around our necks we waded across three rivers. Crossing the first we smashed the ice to get across, but by the time we reached the third the water was distinctly tepid. So was my face. With the wind and sun my lips and nose had cracked open and blood was oozing out. For lunch we huddled in the shade of a sand-dune and opened a tin of tuna fish. I rubbed the oil on my sores, realising that I was probably only adding cooking oil to the frying pan, but for the time being it relieved the pain.

Just before dusk we arrived at the strange village of Chipaya, situated somewhere in the middle of that vast desert plain. Small round huts of adobe bricks, thatched with coarse desert grass, sprouted from the sand. Brown leathery faces peered out of the doorways of those windowless homes as we swerved in amongst them, wondering what our reception would be like. We did not have to wait long to find out.

An extrovert man flagged us down and in Spanish invited us into his house. Things looked pretty good, but as soon as we were inside, his amicable hospitable tone changed and it was down to business. He was the mayor he told us and before he would let us penetrate further into the village, or for that matter return from whence we had come, we must make a 'voluntary' contribution to the community. Neither of us very much liked the idea of being held captive by the ruler of the village, but nor did we feel free to part with 300 precious pesos to line that greedy man's pocket. Marcello and I had a quick mutter to each other and came up with an idea. Yes we were very willing to make a contribution to the village, but we had hired the bicycles in Sabaya and had left our money there as security. The mayor was not pleased at this at all, but quickly came up with a remedy to the problem. When we returned, he would send men with us to Sabaya to collect the money. That at least delayed the problem and would allow us to escape the clutches of this village tyrant. Not wanting to lose our 'goodwill' and maybe jeopardise his prospect financial gain, he allowed us to sleep in the 'Town Hall'. We cleared the rubbish and filth from a patch of the mud floor and between sacks of soya corn donated by the USA, lay down to ponder our predicament and sleep.

After a breakfast of bread and water and under the ever watchful eye of the mayor, we walked around the village. The sun was just rising, biting into the intense cold and streaming through the now open doors of those unique huts. Every door in the village faced the rising sun. Similar to the huts of the

Navaho Indians, whose doorways, for religious reasons always faced east.

The inhabitants, much darker than the normal indigenous Bolivians peered back at us unspeaking as they began their daily chores. The women and girls, barefoot, their hair braided, wore black or brown, coarse, woollen, loose fitting garments. The men and boys were dressed uniformly in black woollen trousers, white and brown striped ponchos with a belt around the waist. Little coloured caps with ear flaps could just be seen beneath large white woven dome-shaped hats. The coloured caps were the only bit of clothing not obviously made locally, everything else it would seem being totally unique to that village.

Later when I had returned to Sabaya, the schoolmaster there came out with an interesting comment. "Those people in Chipaya are not like us, they are not from here, they are from North America." That was an intriguing thought, but he could tell me no more. I felt there was definitely a ring of truth in that tantalising comment, for yes, their skin colouration and facial bone structure bore a striking resemblance to those of the North American Indians I have seen. It would seem from the schoolmaster's attitude that although they had lived there for centuries, (which was apparent from the fact that few of them speak Spanish, but a language similar to the ancient and almost extinct Uru) he still considered them intruders, foreigners and best left in their self-sufficient isolation.

Marcello knew that somewhere near the village was a lake supporting interesting bird life, presumably the remains of what once covered the entire plain. With the hope of escaping we both became instant ornithologists. No, the mayor did not like the idea at all, but not wanting to alienate us and risk a reduced 'contribution', he forced a grin and continued the charade of hospitality. He would accompany us. Once clear of the village we accelerated at top speed, the mayor grimly struggling to keep pace. We were struggling too, but were not going to show it. After an hour the mayor somewhat puffed out and fed up with his youthful charges announced that we were turning back. In mock surprise we dissented, saying we hadn't seen the lake yet. Clear of his village and without his henchmen there was nothing he could do. He turned back while we carried on, assuring him that we would return by nightfall. We did, but not to Chipaya.

For another hour we cycled on, free, happy and at a reduced speed, until we reached the muddy shores of Salar de Coipasa and a sight weird enough for a space fiction film. Multitudes of flamingos flocked around the shallows of the lake. Beyond the lake and muddy, yellow, brown, white, salt-encrusted plain, the jagged white peaks of the Andes pierced the steel-blue sky. For miles across that bleak barren world with its numerous rivulets meandering into the lake, were hundreds of mud brick beehive huts. A silent city abandoned. A flock of flamingos circling silently in the distance was the only movement within the boundaries of the horizon.

I left my clogged up bicycle and squelched my way to the nearest hut.

The mud sucked the heel off my boot and like one of the flamingos I stood on one leg on that eerie moonscape and looked in vain for a rock to hammer it back on with. We stooped and entered the black hole which served as both door and window. The walls tapering up to a hole in the centre of the roof were black with soot. An earthenware cooking pot lay where the fire would have been. But with a fire in the centre of the floor it would not have been possible for anyone to lie down straight, the hut was so small. Rather like sleeping inside an old-fashioned chimney. What would they have found to burn? Perhaps once coarse tufts of grass and hard moss grew there, but as the llamas ate it, the people had no choice but to abandon their homes for pastures new.

We dragged our mud clogged bikes to a river, dunked them, then rode off back towards Sabaya, giving Chipaya a wide berth on the way. Eight hours later as the sun went down, we rode up to the familiar bar for a much needed beer. There we found the mayor, who very kindly let us use his 'office' to sleep in. A totally different character from the one we had so recently escaped from.

We awoke to find ourselves confined to barracks once again. It was national census day and no one, including us, was allowed to leave their homes. It was quite amusing to watch from the doorway, as the older inhabitants, who presumably found it difficult to accept such pointless governmental interference, sneaked out of their homes to attend to their flocks. But it was no use, they were escorted back protesting loudly. At least there was no likelihood of the mayor of Chipaya's henchmen arriving on the scene, though I feel that if they had, their reception would have been rather cool, for the mayor and schoolteacher were horrified when we told them what had happened. It was the schoolteacher who came to add our details to the census. About twenty intrigued spectators also squeezed in, to make a party of it and watch the fun as two gringos tried in vain to answer complicated questions in Spanish.

A lorry arrived outside the bar the following morning, destined for the city of Oruro. The driver told us it would leave at 11 a.m., so we were delighted when we rumbled out of Sabaya at 2 p.m., only three hours late. During the afternoon as we bumped our way over the rock strewn Altiplano I had a bout of dysentery. First the feet go numb, a cold sweat sweeps over you, then you can't wait any longer. A shout of "stop the lorry", vault over the side and trousers down in one swift motion so to speak. Very humiliating squatting there with absolutely no cover and a lorry full of Indians watching, who think it's all highly amusing. Just as well they don't have much of a sense of privacy. However, the amusement did wear a bit thin after the fourth stop.

Previously I had been desperately cold and uncomfortable while travelling by lorry at night, so a different course of action was called for. As daylight faded I burrowed into the centre of the heap of bodies, like a wren in winter-time. But I overheated, was crushed and very nearly suffocated. Seems there is no way of winning. What did annoy us though, was the way the lorry kept stopping for the driver to have a few hours' sleep in the warm cab, while everyone in the back froze. We eventually arrived at Oruro just before dawn, tired, stiff and painfully cold.

Knowing that the road joining the cities of Oruro and La Paz was the busiest and best in the country, Marcello and I tried a bit of hitching. After two hours we had not seen a single private vehicle, so we gave in and caught a bus. Not one car did we see on that 300 kilometre stretch of road. I didn't land a single free hitch in the whole of my time in Bolivia. That was something pretty unique in my experience.

After a couple of days revelling in the civilisation of La Paz, we both agreed that we ought to see another side of Bolivian life and visit the lowlands or Yungas.

At the city frontier the police, for some reason best known to themselves, ordered the protesting Bolivians out from the back of the truck. Strangely the two gringos were allowed to stay on board.

The rough road climbed up through eucalyptus groves, up and up, past a landscape mistakable for remotest Highland Scotland in winter-time. A statue of Christ at 4,725 metres altitude, blasted by snow and icy winds, over-shadowed by gigantic rugged snow-clad peaks, marked the end of an hour-long climb. Before us the ribbon of road wriggled in hairpin bends, down, down to infinity. With the push of gravity behind it, the truck rattled and swayed unnervingly past a few grass thatched stone huts, down into a gorge, the speeding wheels perilously close to the cliff dropping perpendicular to the jungle far beneath us. We crawled from the sanctuary of our cold sleeping bags and breathed in the warm fragrance of verdant foliage.

Dropped off at a road junction, we walked on, the late afternoon sun filtering down the tree-covered mountain side, flickering on the road beneath. Everywhere were flowers, bananas and oranges. I picked one and thought back only four hours, when we were huddled in the back of the truck, our teeth chattering, amongst a bleak landscape of bare rock and snow. How pleasant it was to sit by a fire amongst the darkening shadows, listening to the ripple of a nearby stream, wallowing in the luxury of our first warm evening in Bolivia.

On arrival, by cattle truck, at the rather squalid concrete and corrugated iron town of Chulumani, we were intrigued to find Negroes living there. It seemed somehow odd to see Negro women dressed in bowler hats and full skirts, like the native Bolivians.

After a much needed meal of tripe and potatoes in a ramshackle café (it's potatoes with everything in Bolivia), we hitched on. The lorry stopped for two hours to pick up stones, then another hour to unload and yet a further stop to fill up a hole in the road.

The next one stopped for an hour to pick up coffee beans, then a stop for coca leaves. Most of the Bolivian coca is grown in that area and it is from the leaves of the plant that cocaine is extracted. We sat on the enormous hessian sacks of leaves, chewing happily. I feel that the driver must have been getting 'high' on coca too, for suddenly on seeing a truck ahead of him he accelerated. The race was on. The lorries swerved violently from side to side as we attempted to pass, while the other driver tried to prevent us. Whoever was in front would be the one to pick up any waiting fare paying passengers. The Bolivians with us in the back became very quiet, reconciled to their fate, for the race was downhill along the side of a ravine, a vertical drop from the edge of the narrow winding rock strewn road. I climbed out of the lorry and hung on the back. If that maniac was hell bent on suicide, I might just have a chance of jumping clear.

Encamped again by a river, the birds' evening chorus resembled hundreds of little electric motors in need of oiling. Everywhere was an amazing selection of highly coloured bird life, but the little green parrots were the most charming of all. At daybreak we awoke to a different chorus, that of cocks crowing and sheep bleating.

For two more days, we travelled around the Yungas, before parting company. Marcello wanted to linger longer in that paradise, while I felt it was time to move on.

Leaving the little town of Corico in a lorry bound for La Paz, I could not but feel a bit sad at leaving such a charming place. Rough cobbled streets, rather smelly, but with a peaceful feeling of timeless decay. Beyond, impressive forest-clad wrinkled mountains.

For the fourth and last time I arrived in La Paz. Bolivia seems to be unique in that respect. Wherever you want to go in the country you have to first return to the central hub, before branching out along another spoke of the wheel.

At dawn a couple of days later I managed to locate a bus leaving for Copacabana. As soon as we reached the middle of absolutely nowhere, the bus gave a few coughs and spluttered to a stop. As the men indulged in their usual custom of urinating all over the side of the bus, the driver removed the carburettor and to my horror dismantled it in the middle of the sandy road. I watched in despair as bored passengers crowded around the driver with 'helpful' suggestions, while scuffling sand over the numerous minute, but vital parts of the carburettor. It seemed like a miracle when the driver relocated the bits, reassembled it and after the incredibly short stop of only one hour, we were rumbling off across the Altiplano once more.

Copacabana lies on the shore of lake Titicaca, snuggled in a hollow between terraced hills. The dry, faded patchwork colours of the fields, the terraces and the eucalyptus groves set in a clear warm climate is enchantingly beautiful. As the bus had passed along the shore of the lake I had seen many of the reed boats unique to Titicaca, but at Copacabana there were none to be seen. The inhabitants of the town seemed to be more opulent than most, for instead, they had fishing boats not unlike Yorkshire cobles. The town did not seem short of modern amenities either. Even the room I booked into had the luxury of electric light, though no switch. Contact was made in the usual way of twisting together two bare wires which hung down from the ceiling.

The following morning was Sunday and outside the cathedral an extremely colourful and noisy service was in progress. A dilapidated assortment of old lorries and bicycles, all decked in ribbons, were being blessed by the priest. Fireworks were thrown in all directions, then the vehicles were baptised by having beer bottles smashed over them.

Outside the town a score or more men and women were sitting in a field drinking. They called me over to watch my reactions as I drank the liquor they offered me. We all laughed together, the communual language for non-linguists. The men in Bolivia are easy enough to laugh and converse with but the women were much more serious and less approachable.

The bus for Peru stopped at the border and waited, as I, the only 'extranjero' on board had my passport checked and filled in a form declaring how much money I had. That is to try and prevent money being changed on the black market. When you leave the country, money remaining, plus receipts of money changed at the bank, should all tally.

On arriving soon after at the town of Yunguyo, I had to report to the immigration office. It was a great relief when my passport was stamped and I was not asked to produce a ticket ensuring transport out of Peru. The law demands an onward or return ticket, but I had neither.

Sunday was festival day in Yunguyo. The plaza was packed with market stalls selling everything from cloth to ironmongery. Bands and dancers dressed in the most gaudy costumes imaginable paraded the streets as if competing one against another. The ancient haunting music of Inca pipes could be heard amongst lorry horns and modern brass bands.

On board the lorry bound for the city of Puno were a most unusual number of gringos. Two Germans, two Argentinians, and a Brazilian. In Brazil I had been known as a gringo, but there, even the Brazilian was referred to as one. Every 'extranjero' seems to be a gringo to the natives, although the term should apply only to people of British descent and North Americans.

For six hours we skirted around the lake, past mud brick houses roofed with corrugated iron or thatch. Beyond the cattle and sheep pastures and plots of arable land, were terraced hillsides. Some were still in use, but many had obviously been abandoned generations ago. Frequently we stopped to be checked out by bored policemen, or to pick up an ever increasing number of passengers. The truck became incredibly crowded and we all had to stand to fit in. Even then we arrived at Puno with a dozen or more people hanging on to the outside as well.

Puno was the most sordid and unimpressive place I had so far seen in South America. The foreshore of the lake which could be an asset to the city, is instead a vast sprawling rubbish tip and public lavatory. Scrawny dogs scavenged amongst the rubbish, then turned to attack when I went too close. With my back to the wall and thoughts of rabies, I desperately fought them off with stones, until after what seemed like an endless eternity they slunk away.

It was with a sigh of relief that I left the city the following morning. The bus passed through sparsely populated uninteresting green mountains, then over a dusty stony desert. There in the desert were some salt lakes, where by evaporation, people were collecting little piles of salt. Then we skirted the snow-capped perfect cone of El Misti. Beyond the incredibly beautiful dormant volcano, the road wound down like a crumpled ribbon thrown carelessly on the ground, in to the valley and so to Arequipa.

With a population of about a quarter of a million, Arequipa is the third largest city in Peru. But somehow size and commercialism has not ruined the beauty of it. In the vicinity of the lovely colonnaded plaza are many ancient churches, magnificent mansions and quaint old Spanish style buildings. All of them built of 'sillar', a most beautiful white volcanic stone which shines in the sun — and in Arequipa, there is plenty of sun. It supposedly shines for 360 days of the year. Combined with a rainfall of about one inch annually, Arequipa must have about the most delightful climate in the world.

After much tramping around the streets and haggling over prices, I paid for lodgings in the cheapest place I could find, I found myself sharing a room with a most amicable young Peruvian, who insisted on taking me out to eat in the market. Even at 10 p.m. market stalls were still in business. Women were huddled over primus stoves amongst the rubbish at the edge of the road, cooking up all sorts of food to sell. Just the same as in Bolivian cities. The women even dressed the same, except that they did not wear bowler hats. That seems to be a custom unique to Bolivia.

The colonnaded plaza, El Misti looming over the city and Santa Catalina convent, are what impressed me most in Arequipa. The convent was for centuries a closed and secretive world, a walled town within a city. A population of about 500 nuns and 2,000 unpaid female servants lived out their lives without ever leaving the sanctuary of those walls. Today, the few nuns who remain there live in seclusion in one small part of the convent. The rest, which is now open to the public is a maze of narrow cobbled streets, cloisters, kitchens, simple houses and a church. All of it built in the beautiful white volcanic stone and hardly changed since its construction centuries ago. It's a charming town, isolated from the twentieth century. A peaceful tranquil jewel plucked from the past.

Once clear of the city the bus headed out across a vast wilderness of sand and rocks, interspersed by a few lush green valleys. Three hours later, after surprisingly coming through a landscape of green rolling hills covered in mauve and yellow flowers, we reached the Pacific coast and the rather scruffy town of Camaña.

As we lurched to a stop on the pot-holed road, women and children clambered on to the bus to sell bread and bananas. Posters advertising the drink 'Inca Cola' seemed to be stuck on nearly every squalid building. Just about enough to make any proud full blooded Inca turn in his grave. At Camaña we joined the Pan American Highway, our speed increasing dramatically as we sped northwards along that fine tarmacked toll road. On our left, mile upon mile of desert beach was lapped by the blue Pacific ocean. On our right, gigantic sand-dunes towered hundreds of feet above us. Occasionally rivers broke through the dunes supporting a populated oasis along their banks.

At 6 a.m. we arrived at the capital city of Lima, having been woken up and well checked out by the police an hour previously. Very soon I found myself in the central square or Plaza de Armas. Along one side of the plaza were iron railings, behind which stood the imposing Government Palace. Even at that time in the morning, soldiers in black and red uniforms were doing a high stepping guard change.

Within the plaza was a large bronze statue of Francisco Pizarro mounted on his horse. Proud, larger than life, Pizarro was depicted as the hero. In a chapel just inside the entrance to the cathedral, still in sight of the magnificent statue, lay the body of the conquistador in a glass coffin. A reminder of the mortality of man, hero or not. Though how a man who enslaved and slaughtered a whole civilisation in his lust for gold, ends up with pride of place in a consecrated cathedral beats me.

I spent a few days in Lima exploring the city, 'home' for that time being a mattress, along with rows of others, on the floor of a lodging house. John and Tony who I had met at Tiahuanaco, seemed pleased to see me again and agreed to show me around the city. Travelling jam packed on a bus reminded me of a time when I had once had my pocket picked. I related the incident to my two friends as light conversation. Things were not so humorous when we stepped off the bus though, for John found his wallet missing, along with over eighty pounds. It must have happened as I was actually talking about pickpockets, which left me with a horrible feeling, for ever since I have wondered if they thought that I did it.

There are many museums in Lima, but the museum of the Inquisition is probably the most unique and bizarre. It was there that the 'Court of Inquisition' was held from 1570-1820. The lifelike re-creation of tortures of times past, shows the inhumanity done to man in the name of religion. It's the spine chilling reminder of such atrocities that makes me feel glad to live in the twentieth century. But then this century also has cracks in its veneer of civilisation, even in Lima. That evening I met John and Tony in the suburb of Miraflores, for a couple of drinks. When the bill came, we had exactly the right amount between us, with just enough left over for our bus fares – to the exact solace. That made us sweat a bit, for there was not enough time left to walk. From 1 a.m. to 5 a.m. there was a curfew. Any civilian found on the streets between those hours was liable to be shot!

In the 'museum of anthropology and archaeology', were many naturally mummified bodies from the Paracas culture of 1300 BC. I found it intriguing to notice, that unlike the native occupants I have seen in South America, who all had black hair, those mummies had red hair. Their burial pots also showed pictures of men with stretchers in their ear lobes. Both features are in common with the megalithic and mysterious statues of Easter Island. Is there a connection? But to where have all the descendants of those red headed people vanished?

The next day, twenty-five kilometres further on down the coast from Lima, I pulled out of the sand a human skull and thigh bone. With the skull in my hand, like Hamlet, I mused again on the mysteries of Peru's intriguing past cultures. Would our civilisation one day be just a curiosity, like that skull buried in the sand by the ghost of a crumbling mud brick pyramid? That monstrous pile of derelict bricks in a sandy desert, was once a glittering temple to the sun. In 1533 Pizarros' brother arrived at Pachacámac, the then largest city on the coast. He looted the already 200-year-old temple and killed the priests, so putting yet another nail in the coffin of one of the world's most incredible civilisations.

Peru − Sacrificial stone, Machu Picchu

CHAPTER 5

PAST MYSTERIES AND PRESENT PREDICAMENTS

At Chavin, high up in the Andes, are the remains of a civilisation of great antiquity. The temple ruins there supposedly date from over 8,000 years ago! The bus for Chavin left Lima in the early afternoon. It passed through the ever-growing slums which surround the capital city, then followed the coast, past vast sand-dunes (or mountains covered in sand) some exceeding 1,000 feet in height. Occasionally we passed through flat fertile irrigated valleys, where maize, sugar-cane and vegetables seemed to be the predominant crop. At Pativilca the bus turned off the fast smooth coastal road and began its slow rough climb, up into the sub zero altitudes of barren stony mountains.

At four in the morning the bus gave a violent lurch and crunched to a stop at a drunken angle, spilling its sleeping passengers into chaotic panic. We scambled out as best we could, to find that the back wheel had slipped off the edge of a narrow plank bridge. The bus overhung at a dizzy angle, a perpendicular drop to eternity. Some men huddled around the back of the bus in the dim pre dawn light and tried to jack it back on to the road. It fell off the jack and slithered nearer to the point of no return. Meanwhile, wrapped in my sleeping bag, I was leaping around the mountainside like a chamois, trying without success to keep warm.

Lo and behold, just as dawn broke another bus came along that mountain road. Armed with picks and shovels (every bus carried such essential equipment), we all set to and carved from the precipice enough room for the other bus to pass. Then we all clambered on to the serviceable bus, leaving the driver and his cronies behind to ponder over a nigh impossible anti-gravitational problem. But we also had to leave our luggage behind, as it was all stowed on the roof of the endangered bus. The driver was adamant that we should not try and retrieve it, as the extra weight of a man on the roof might be all that was needed to topple it past the point of no return.

A couple of hours later and still wondering if I should ever see my luggage again, we drove into the village of Chavin, set by a river in a rugged picturesque valley. Just outside the present day village is a large square sunken arena, with flights of stone steps leading down to it. Close by is a smaller circular one. Beside these are overgrown mounds of stone, giving little indication of their previous shape or use.

The exterior view of all this seemed rather disappointing, but that was not all. In the side of one of those humps of stone was a square black hole. Not having a torch, I hired a lantern and crawled inside. Passages went in all directions, but strangely led nowhere. Staring out into that cramped labyrinth were exquisite carved stone heads of symbolic demons. Being entombed they had not fallen victim to the ravages of time and appeared to be in near perfect condition. How long have they been there and for what strange purpose? By their construction, they looked as if they once adorned the temple, in the position of gargoyles.

By midday I had seen all I wanted, but there was still no sign of the bus with my rucksack on it. A lorry was just leaving the village, so along with two Germans who were going the same way, I climbed aboard. The bus was still there, only in a noticeably worse position, due to the vain efforts of the driver. Something had to be done, or I could envisage my waiting for days, or seeing my rucksack vanishing into the chasm.

As the drivers stopped for a chat, the two Germans, while guarding my rear, shouted to the men to pull on a retaining rope. Meanwhile I dashed up the side of the bus, retrieved my rucksack and was then myself hauled off by my feet.

No damage was done so we continued down the rough hairpin roads, leaving the bus to an unknown fate. But strange as it may seem, a very similar fate nearly befell the lorry. A few minutes later we came upon another plank bridge spanning a stream. The road was straight just there, so the driver rattled along at a good speed. As the back wheel reached the timbers there was a tremendous jolt as they snapped a plank which jammed behind the wheels and tore up subsequent ones. Momentum just got us to the other side, but we left a trail of destruction behind, effectively closing the road to any other vehicles.

We passed over a stretch of rough grassland, then down between brown and yellow mountains studded with eucalyptus trees. It was rather attractive in a dry sort of way. Finally at dusk, the lorry arrived at the town of Huaraz.

When travelling in Bolivia on motorised transport, I had no choice but to pay. It had become a habit which had rather spilled over into Peru. Lifts didn't cost much and the temptation of an easy way out was appealing. However, on counting my money and knowing that I still had the best part of 20,000 kilometres travelling to do in South America, I realised that it was a luxury I could not afford. Whereas in Bolivia private vehicles were non-existent, in Peru there were precious few, but there were some, so from then on I resolved to rely, if possible, on hitching.

After a breakfast of bread and water, I walked up the rough steep road past eucalyptus trees, past small brown dusty fields and adobe huts, where chickens scratched at the dust in the open doorways.

A lorry stopped for me, where a group of soldiers were busy repairing a similar bridge to the one we had destroyed the previous day. For one and a half hours that lorry laboriously struggled from side to side up hairpin bends, to the bitter winds of a snow-covered pass. Behind, the town of Huaraz was still visible far below us, while ahead lay the distant Pacific.

For two and a half more hours we rattled snake-like down a zigzag track into the tropics. Banana trees grew beside the road, while gigantic candelabra like cactus (some five metres high), speckled dry green across white rocky, limestone mountains. Another two hours took us through a bleak mountainous moonscape, then down through a fertile plain to Casma.

A car, the first since Brazil, then gave me a lift down to the coast, to the sprawling, squalid, industrial city of Chimbote.

A desert of filth, excrement and sand bordered the city. There, finding a building under construction, I clambered up on to the flat roof for the night, out of reach of the scavenging dogs which roam the outskirts of most South American cities. Lying in the gathering dusk and plummeting temperatures, I mused on the fact that never before had I seen such a variety of landscapes and climates in the course of one day.

At dawn, it was back to the Pan American Highway. It's a good road with a reasonable amount of traffic, so after only two hours of walking I hitched a lift which took me all the way to Trujillo, just two hours further on up the desert coast.

About three miles from the city, close to the Pacific shore, but rising from the flat desert sands are the magnificently imposing ruins of Chan Chan. Crumbling though still monstrous, adobe walls rise five to seven metres out of the desert, silent sentinels to yet another long lost civilisation. All morning in the burning sun, I walked around what must be nearly 25 square kilometres of crumbling temples, streets, houses, palaces and city walls. All of it built of mud, some still preserved well enough to make out moulded decorations of rows of fish and pelicans.

Legend has it that the Incas invaded that imperial city of the gigantic Chimú empire in about A.D. 1400. All they had to do in fact was cut off the water supply which was brought by canals from the distant mountains and wait. Then it rained, a remarkable event in the Atacama desert, which is the driest place in the world. One hundred and fifty years later, the Spaniards entered the abandoned city and dug up the burial mounds, looting them of their gold and silver ornaments. Soon after it rained again, for the second and last time. It is the result of those two rainstorms over a period of nearly six hundred years, that has dissolved so much of Chan Chan.

A walk of about eight kilometres took me through an area of well irrigated land, where extensive crops of sugar-cane were being grown. Towering high above the flat plain and visible for miles, were the huge Moche pyramids, the Huaca del Sol and the Huaca de la Luna. The Huaca del Sol, or temple to the sun, built of countless millions of adobe bricks is truly vast. For sheer bulk, it looks as if it outstrips the Great Pyramid in Egypt.

A stream which now runs past the pyramid, was once diverted by the Spaniards, so as to erode away the walls of the Huaca. Presumably someone was always on watch to see if any treasure rooms were revealed by the constant erosion. Consequently about one third of the pyramid was washed away, but whatever was found and melted down remains a mystery.

From Trujillo I wanted to go up into the Andes again, to Cajamarca, the site of the annihilation of the Inca civilisation. In order to get clear of the city on the right road, I caught a bus for a few miles to a road junction, high up on a rugged and bleak mountainside where cactus and the bitter wind were my only company. The climate had once again totally changed in just a few miles, due to the altitude, I had forgotten to squeeze the air out of my plastic waterbottle and now it was all blown up and leaking, due to the fall in air pressure.

If you want to stay alive in South America, never bring out a wad of money and peel off notes in public. So each morning, in one of my pockets I put as much money as I thought I might need that day. As I watched the bus disappearing in a cloud of dust, it was best that I was alone, for I felt in a murderous state of mind. My daily allowance was gone, someone on that bus had picked my pocket.

Some hours later a ministry of agriculture truck took me to the village of Otuzco. There a woman very kindly took me to the police post and asked them if they would try and organise a lift for me. I was invited in to sit down and wait, then at midday one of the policemen took me to a café for lunch, which was most hospitable of him, reviving my faith in a people who I had come to regard as a nation of pickpockets. Meals in Peruvian cafés seem to be almost without exception, the same: tasteless watery soup with a chunk of bone or inedible gristle in it. This is followed by a plate of boiled rice, under-done boiled potatoes and another piece of bone or gristle. The second part of the meal being exceedingly dry and difficult to swallow.

During the afternoon I sat at the table in the otherwise practically barren whitewashed room and drank pisco with the police chief. "To keep out the cold," he said, then laughed.

At nine in the evening the first vehicle of the day, a lorry, rumbled its way through the village. The driver pulled up outside the police post for the usual compulsory document check, then the police talked him in to giving me a lift. They were all smiles as I clambered on to the load of disgustingly dirty drums of oil and petrol. I did not want to appear ungracious, but I was not happy about it and rather wished the lorry had never come, as I knew what was in store for me. With nowhere to lie down, I sat on top of the oily cab, totally exposed to the wind and plummeting temperatures of night. The lorry crawled for hour upon hour at about 8 m.p.h. along an abominably rough road, to well up above the snow line. With sleeping bag upside down over my head, I shivered my way through yet another unbelievably uncomfortable sleepless night.

As dawn broke the lorry rattled into the plaza at Huamachuco. Numb with cold, I staggered off down the road past a few early risers, well wrapped up from the still sub zero temperatures. I kept walking until the sun was high in the sky and the warmth had penetrated to my bones.

The countryside was enchantingly romantic. Lakes, streams, groups of trees, mountains and moorland. They were all there mixed together and with the reds, greens, yellows and brown of the fields, it was some of the most attractive scenery I have ever seen. Lying there dozing in the warm sunshine, made the previous night seem like an imaginary nightmare.

Early in the afternoon, a plume of dust in the distance heralded the first vehicle to come my way. Thankfully the pick up truck stopped and took me the six hour journey to the town of Cajamarca, set in a pleasant valley at the base of a line of hills.

It was there in the plaza in 1532, that Pizarro ambushed the Inca chieftain Atahualpa. The Inca guards, strangely unarmed, were slaughtered, while Atahualpa was captured. The Inca promised in return for his freedom, to have a room filled with gold. The room was filled, but regardless of this, Atahualpa was killed. Pizarro then marched on the Inca capital of Cuzco and sacked the city.

Sitting on a bench in the plaza, surrounded by box hedges cut into the shape of heads, jugs and men on horseback, all the while being pestered by shoeshine boys, it was difficult to imagine that bloody slaughter four hundred and fifty years ago. Overlooking the plaza was the cathedral, begun only a hundred years after that slaughter, but not completed until 1960.

A short walk took me to the Cuarto de Rescate or ransom chamber. That room, solidly built of cut limestone blocks, was the one Atahualpa had filled with gold, to the depth that his hand would reach. I measured the room as seven paces wide and twelve and a half long.

The twisting rough road from Cajamarca took me over dry brown mountains. The driver of the truck I was hitching in, told me that those same hills would all be green when the December rains started, though it was hard to believe it on that October day.

Once over the top, the road descended through steep valleys, barren except for cacti and tarantula spiders, my driver informed me. On down past caves where vampire bats lived, down to the fertile tropics where papaw, mangoes, bananas, rice and maize grew.

Travelling once more on the Pan American Highway up the Pacific coast, the landscape changed sharply to one of sandy desert, or a vast beach, depending on which way you like to look at it. Occasionally the monotony was broken by small towns, situated in fertile valleys where rivers flowed into the Pacific.

At Lambayeque the road turned inland through scraggy bushland, infested with goats trying constantly to turn that area into a total desert as well. Further north, nodding donkeys pumped for oil from beneath the sandy wastes, while along the desert coast, rough fishing villages of corrugated iron and drift wood supplied factories with fish to be pulverised into fertiliser.

As soon as I crossed the border into Ecuador, two days' hitching from Cajamarca, the country changed dramatically to green fields and forest. A forest of peculiar green bottle-shaped trees with feathery tendrils. Until the oil boom of 1972, bananas were the chief export of Ecuador, and as the road penetrated further north, the landscape became almost exclusively banana plantations.

I had come from the driest place on Earth to one of the wettest. Even the tiled, or leaf thatched houses of wood or split bamboo, were built on stilts to keep the water out. I had a feeling that it was going to rain that night. It did, with a vengeance, and I was glad I had decided to part with 50 sucres, for a night in a room of rough hewn wooden planks with a reasonably rain-proof roof. Actually it had been a big decision, for 50 sucres was equivalent to about one pound. That was far more than I had been accustomed to pay for a night's lodging and more than I could really afford. But Ecuador was to prove to be far more expensive than Peru or Bolivia.

Before setting out in the morning I decided to live it up and go into a café for a breakfast of bread and coffee. When it came to pay, it appeared that the café proprietor had given it to me. It's some small gesture like that which starts you off on the right footing in a country. So it was with a much lighter heart that I set off to hitch from the town of Machala to Guayaquil, the largest city in Ecuador.

I anticipated staying in Guayaquil for a few days, so I found a room for 30 sucres in a hotel. Well actually it was a converted warehouse, but it was the cheapest place where I could find a room which appeared safe. There was no window, which was an asset, as at least no one could climb in. From a long frayed electric flex, a light bulb hung in the centre of the whitewashed room. Two wires with bare ends also hung from the ceiling. It was simply a matter of joining those two wires to get a light. That can be a slightly hazardous procedure in the pitch dark. The only other furnishing in the room, besides the cockroaches, alive and dead, was a simple iron bedstead. On the outside of the door was a hasp with a padlock. This I exchanged for my own lock, which I carried expressly for the purpose. Then at least I knew no one else had a spare key! I don't describe that room because it was exceptional. Quite the reverse, it was the sort of room I usually slept in when I paid for lodgings in South America, so it is for its normality that I describe it.

My reason for going to Guayaquil was in the hope of finding a way to the Galapagos Islands, 1,000 kilometres west. Once unburdened of my rucksack, I set off to try and find out the cheapest way to the islands.

No sooner had I stepped out into the street, than I found myself amongst a mob of students. Before I had time to realise what was going on and get out of the way, tear gas bombs went off and the police charged in. Discretion being the better part of valour, I scarpered at a quick rate of knots. Such was my first encounter with Guayaquil.

I had been warned by a driver I was hitching with, that the city was notorious and I soon found that to be true. Very soon I noticed a number of watch straps lying on the ground. Quickly I took my watch off and hid it away, I didn't want it wrenched off my wrist. Days later I met two girls who had been on the receiving end of that game. One had her handbag snatched, while another had her ear-ring ripped out, both in broad daylight.

Also on my first day in the city I saw two youths trying to break into a car. They saw me watching them, gave a sheepish grin, but when I moved on they carried on with their crime. The street was full of people but no one seemed to notice, no one wanted to know.

Two days later another riot erupted without warning near me and I was given another taste of tear gas and charging police.

On another occasion a fire engine screeched to a halt by me, just as I was about to explore a rather intriguing back street. A fireman jumped off the engine and told me not to go into the street as I probably would not come out alive. I was amazed and grateful that a fire engine in full flight should stop to warn a gringo of such dangers, but appalled that such blatant vice should exist. Shocked as I was by all this, the full realisation of it did not hit me, until on a later visit to Guayaquil I was personally to suffer.

However, continuing my quest for a cheap way to the Galapagos, I eventually tracked down the military airport on the outskirts of the city. The guard at the gate understandably said no and would not let me in. I persisted and eventually a superior officer, who spoke excellent English, took me along to the administration office. There I was told that there was a possibility of my obtaining a lift in the military plane, but the man who dealt with such matters was away, there being a fiesta in progress.

Three days later I tracked down the 'man who deals with such matters', only to be told that I should have to go to my embassy in the capital Quito, first. They might, on my behalf contact the Ministry of Defence, who could then authorise me to travel with the military.

It was a chance I was not going to miss, so the following morning I hitched off on the road to Quito. Well actually it was not quite that simple for I had the greatest difficulty in finding the way out of the city. Whenever I asked people the way they invariably directed me back to the bus station. I know there was a language problem, but people seemed unable to listen or pay any regard to my frantic sign language of tapping my boots. It certainly added miles of foot slogging around the city streets. Once found, the road led me out of town past the most hideous cemetery I've yet seen. Multi-storey, high rise blocks of concrete tombs stand stark against the skyline. Black holes gape ready to receive a coffin and a concrete slab to seal up another high-rise 'flat'.

The road to Quito lay through scrubby bush or marshy fields, both equally unattractive, except for the flocks of snow-white stork-like birds that I had previously seen in Amazonas. The towns were no better, with their mixture of old thatched wooden buildings, new concrete ones, telegraph wires, advertising signs, decay and rubbish. They had no artistic value whatsoever. In fact it was just plain ugly chaos.

The country became more thickly forested as we travelled along the old colonial road to the rough wooden houses of Santo Domingo. Within the vicinity of Santo Domingo is the intriguing tribe of Colorado Indians. They cut off all their hair, except for a central strip. This they dye red, then putting gum on it, thatch or plait it into a sort of hard hat. The result is distinctly curious.

From the forested lowlands, the car I was travelling in, a fast and powerful one, climbed steadily upwards for two hours. Up above the tree line to where only stunted bushes and rough grass could be seen through the thick fog. Once over the top, the road led downwards to Quito, the world's second highest capital city.

Walking around the city in the gathering dusk, I was amazed to see so many rats. With every footstep I took they seemed to scamper out from beneath the filth and rubbish which covered the alley-ways. On returning to the plaza I was stunned to see an Indian woman, cooking over a brazier what appeared to be rats on sticks, teeth, ears, feet, everything. Later with some relief, I was to learn that they were not rats but guinea pigs, which are considered to be something of a delicacy.

Having arrived in Quito on a Friday evening, the embassy could not be contacted until the Monday. So on Saturday morning I hitched north to the pleasant old colonial town of Ibarra with its white houses and straight cobbled roads. *En route*, a car with three North American tourists stopped to ask me the way. It ended up with them giving me a lift and taking me out to lunch at an expensive hotel, for the sort of meal I had only dreamed about since leaving England.

In the afternoon I intended to hitch further north, purely for curiosity sake, but after walking a couple of miles out of Ibarra, I found an English style green grassy bank by a gurgling stream. I got no further, it was no good, I just had to sit on it, even if it did make me feel a bit homesick. So with a full stomach and a little gentle cooling rain falling on the otherwise warm sunny day, I dozed off to sleep. It was bliss and made me realise what lovely things we take for granted and pass by without noticing in our rush for living.

The following day I returned to Quito via the same delightful green rounded mountains dotted with eucalyptus trees. In the lower areas were plantations of avocado pears, dairy farms and an abundance of vegetation, already lush, although the rainy season had hardly begun.

Twenty-five kilometres short of Quito the road crosses the Equator. Here by the side of the road is a concrete model of the Earth, one and a half metres or so in diameter.

The word *mañana* crops up rather a lot in that continent and with most days seemingly a festival or holiday, one has to be exceedingly patient and determined in order to conduct any official business. Eventually though, I was put in touch with an English Group Captain, who dealt with matters military between England and Ecuador. He was extremely helpful and armed with a letter written by him on my behalf, I tackled the Ecuadorian Ministry of Defence. A couple of days later I learned that my application had been accepted and the Minister had given his approval for me to travel on the military aircraft. It had taken a week, but it was well worth the wait and of course meanwhile, gave me a chance to see a lot of Quito.

Parts of the old city are quite quaint and picturesque, if you shut your eyes to the filth, telephone wires, cars and buses. The charm of the old colonial houses, packed tight together, is being carefully preserved. All are painted white, with doors, window frames and trimmings a uniform blue. Their wrought iron balconies and overhanging eaves, overshadow the steep winding cobbled streets. That must be a local law, otherwise I can't see everyone conforming.

There were more Indians to be seen in Quito and its vicinity, than in the lowlands. The women wore trilby hats and long skirts, though not full ones as in Bolivia. Some of the women though were dressed in white embroidered skirts and wore gold necklaces, which was most picturesque. The majority of men seemed very drab in second rate westernised clothing, though a few were to be seen with their hair in pigtails and wearing white trousers which terminated about twenty centimetres above the ankle.

Business completed, I washed all my clothes and strung them up in my room, then went to bed early ready for a dawn start south.

I lay there and with amusement watched a number of mice appear from a hole in the wall and scamper across the bare wooden boards. Suddenly without warning the bed shook as the whole room shuddered under the impact of an earthquake. The mice stopped, rooted to the spot, then in a disorientated panic, rushed around the room before disappearing into their hole.

There were four days to wait until the plane was to leave Guayaquil for the Galapagos, so I hitched back by a more picturesque and leisurely route.

Around the village of Baños where I stayed, the landscape was especially beautiful, with the mountains covered with a colourful patchwork quilt of fields. From Baños, the road passed through country not unlike the Highlands of Scotland, except that in parts small irregular unfenced fields had been scratched out of the moorland. Haphazardly dotted around, were little stone or mud thatched huts, each with its own top heavy thatched straw rick. The style of living looked very hard and basic. It was as if I was in a time machine, looking back at a bronze age settlement in the highlands of Britain.

Returning to Guayaquil I once again put up at the same hotel, or converted warehouse as before. I left the hotel next day to have my boots repaired. Only ten minutes was I away, but on returning I found the hasp on my door wrenched off and most of my belongings gone. A few were still left scattered on the floor. Money and passport I always carry with me, day or night, so with them safe it may seem relatively unimportant when a few possessions go missing. But it is not like that when you are thousands of miles from home and what you carry is all you own. Every article is pretty vital to your existence, otherwise you would not have brought it with you in the first place.

Two boys who worked in the hotel stood within view, smirking with much amusement at my distress. That just increased my fury as I interrogated the boys, having the greatest difficulty in restraining myself from throttling the pair of them. One of the boys in pretence of being helpful, though all the time smiling from ear to ear, fetched a hammer and nails for me to repair the door. Incensed at this I flung the hammer the length of the hotel, then confronting the woman who ran the place, demanded that a search was made. She remained seated in her chair totally unruffled by my outburst and flatly refused any co-operation.

While arguing with the old woman, I saw two gringos walk past the entrance. I ran out after them, explained my situation and asked them if they would guard what I believed to be the hotel's only entrance, while I went for the police. Out on the streets I found a policeman and hurriedly explained my problem. He was most unwilling to become involved stating that it was not his department. However he did allow himself to be more or less physically dragged to the scene of the crime. With his backing we searched the hotel and found my things hidden in the bedroom of one of those same two boys.

I was immensely relieved, while everyone else including the policeman were highly amused by the whole affair. The only one not so happy was the culprit who I could cheerfully have murdered and very nearly did before I was restrained by the others. But even he managed a smirk as much as to say, 'well it didn't work this time but there will be plenty more gringos to steal from'.

Still shaking from my experience, I packed my things and moved to another hotel, though by the constant coming and going of clients, I soon discovered that in reality it was a brothel. However, this time I was left undisturbed.

On my previous visit to Guayaquil I had met and conversed with two European lads who were associated with a religious sect known as The Children of God . A couple of hours after my alarming experience at the hotel, I was only too pleased to meet them again in the street. Joining them for a meal that evening at the commune where they lived, I felt the mania for my material possessions somehow seemed very trivial and unimportant, when I saw with what simplicity they lived and with what disinterest they seemed to view all things material. The dignity and calming effect of those people certainly helped to restore the balance of my troubled mind once more. Regardless of their lack of comprehension for my concern for my belongings, they willingly allowed me to leave the majority of my possessions in their safe keeping, for me to collect on my return from the Galapagos. I felt certain that they would be quite safe, as indeed they were.

Galapagos – Marine iguanas on the Island of Santa Cruz

Galapagos – Sea lion on the Island of Plazas

CHAPTER 6

GALAPAGOS – ISLANDS OF EVOLUTION

With the eager anticipation of a day ahead worth remembering, besides the fact it was my birthday, I caught a bus to the airport to catch the 7 a.m. military flight to the Galapagos.

Once in the departure area, I could not help but instantly become aware of a most weird and outrageous character. Edwardo, about 50 years old, dressed in buckskin and ten gallon hat, was reminiscent of something from the early days of the Wild West. Although Ecuadorian, one of his ancestors was from the USA and being extremely proud of this fact, he had to keep up the image. If that was not enough, it very soon became apparent that he was also a loud mouthed immature bore. Such characters repulse me and normally I avoid them at all costs, but on this occasion I did not.

With him was a Canadian girl of roughly the same age as myself. She quietly attached herself to me and pleaded for me to join them. She it seemed, like me, had wanted to find a cheap way to the Galapagos. A mutual friend had arranged for her to travel with Edwardo, as he had influence in the right quarters. Looking at him this seemed hard to believe, but subsequently this proved to be correct, as apparently there were three admirals in his family. Cathy had not actually met him until she arrived at the airport, but was appalled when she did, especially so as he quickly left her in no doubt that he expected 'payment' for the favour. Hence her pleading with me to act as a chaperon to keep him at bay.

For three hours we sat on hard benches along the side of the fuselage, while facing us over piles of equipment were a few inhabitants of the islands on their way home, and some military personnel.

From the rough solitary runway on the island of San Cristóbal, we caught a bus into town, just a very small cluster of wood and corrugated iron houses along the shore. Edwardo made for the naval base which was just outside the town. Here he talked to some officers and within half an hour we were installed in the magnificent and scrupulously clean naval guest quarters. Once settled in and free of the burden of my rucksack I set off on foot to view the island.

The shore is made up of black volcanic boulders, although surprisingly there are numerous little yellow sandy bays. Pelicans patiently waited on the shore line, while blue-beaked and blue-footed gulls dived like arrows for fish. Black crabs sunned themselves, well camouflaged on the black basalt boulders. But as soon as I went any nearer than ten metres they scuttled away. Cautious no doubt for fear of the sea birds which prey on them. Surprisingly out of all the animals I was to see on the islands, it was only the crabs which showed any fear. All the other animals seemed totally unafraid. Can it be that among the larger creatures it is only the crabs which are preyed upon?

Away from the shore, the land is similarly covered by volcanic boulders, between which is a scrubby bushland of cactus, dead white trees and many strange plants which I had never seen before, so giving the place a mysterious enchanting Walt Disney appearance. Forty per cent of plants on the islands are unique to the Galapagos.

Many little lizards sunned themselves on the cinder track, quite oblivious to me as I walked gently upwards to the interior of the island. Altitude brings rain, so the vegetation rapidly changed to banana plantations and grass, on which cattle were grazing.

Later in the evening back at the naval base, we wined and dined in state with the naval commander. He told us that royalty had stayed there for a peaceful retreat on numerous occasions. I can well understand their appreciation of the tranquil serenity of the place.

Edwardo arranged for us to travel by the mail boat to the island of Santa Cruz. So the following morning, after some deliberation, we set off on the seven hour voyage in to the eye of the wind. Frequently the gunwales were under water, as the waves sloshed in to the small open boat, leaving us soaked to the skin within minutes. Passing Barrington Island, seals were bobbing like bottles in the water, watching us watching them. Dolphins escorted us, often playfully leaping across the bows of the boat, within reach of an outstretched hand.

With our feet on dry ground once more, Cathy rid herself of Edwardo, much to his annoyance, forfeiting in the process her free return trip to the mainland. There are civilian flights twice a week to the islands, but at a prohibitively high cost.

In the small village which borders the harbour, Cathy and I found accommodation in the loft of a house. That once arranged, we then had the good fortune to meet up with a Swiss and two French lads. After much haggling, the five of us arranged to hire a boat, so as to spend four days sailing to some of the smaller uninhabited islands.

With supplies bought and a day to wait, the five of us set off along a hardly discernible track, to walk the seven kilometres to Tortuga bay. The rough winding path led through a densely forested lava field. Much of the vegetation was similar to what I had seen on San Cristóbal, except that everywhere there were cactus trees. I had seen many types of cacti before, many large varieties, but nothing like that. Proper timber trees sprouting prickly pear type cactus pads.

The deserted bay, or lagoon as it really is, with cacti crowned cliffs on one side and mangrove swamp on the other, is one of the most beautiful awe-inspiring beaches I have ever seen.

Herons and pelicans fished in the bay, while barking could be heard as seals poked their heads above the water. Crabs scuttled into their holes in the soft white coral sand, while finches, quite unafraid, hopped all over us as we sat or lay still. Scores of black marine iguanas, like miniature rubber dinosaurs, warmed themselves in motionless camouflage on the volcanic rocks. These lizards, unique to the Galapagos, live on brown seaweed which carpets the submerged rocks. Although lung breathing animals, they are able to stay for long periods feeding under water, but eventually have to return to land in order to reheat their bodies. These prehistoric looking creatures, sixty centimetres or more in length, are incidentally the only members of the lizard family who obtain their food from the sea, even to the extent of drinking salt water.

The following morning, we set sail in the twelve metre fishing boat for the small Island of Plazas, two hours away. Sunlight sparkled as flying fish skimmed over the surface of an incredibly blue tranquil sea. Startled and awed we saw monstrous manta rays, two metres and more in length jump from the water and flap across the surface.

Anchoring the boat, we swam to the shore amid sea lions who dived around us in play. One part of the island was covered by sea lions, slithering over the rocks barking. Mothers suckled their pups, while others lay belly upmost blissfully basking in the sun. Walking amongst them they took little notice of us. Certainly there was no sign of fear. Not so the brilliant red and yellow Sally Lightfoot crabs, which scuttled away amongst the rocks at our approach. On the white volcanic rock, cactus trees grow and a fleshy red ground creeping plant which gives the island a most peculiar appearance. Beneath the cactus trees, sea lions lay in the shade, while land iguanas over one metre long, beautifully camouflaged in green and brown, fed on the pads, prickles and all.

Back on the boat with the water gently lapping against the hull, I watched the sun sink below the horizon. Then in the gathering dark of a balmy evening, sprays of sparkling phosphorescent light surrounded the boat, as sea lions played around us. It seemed an incongruous bump back to reality, when a string of French swear words suddenly shattered the tranquillity, to tell us that rats had been ransacking our food stores and rucksacks.

We sailed past towering cliffs of basalt colums as we approached a tiny island only about a hectare in size. Mosquera, an island of fine white coral sand, was home for hundreds of sea lions basking in the sunshine.

The adjoining Island of Seymour is an amazing contrast. In fact the islands seem to be unique in the surprising way they are all completely different. Seymour, dense with white trees, cacti and impenetrable bushes, in parts up to head height, is a haven for nesting birds. Most numerous are the blue-footed boobies which are a member of the cormorant family. There is another less common member of this family found on the islands, which is flightless, its wings only a remnant of what would be needed for use. Many naturalists would have us believe that flightless birds tended to be the ones without enemies, so consequently they lost their need for wings and escape.

Frigate birds, related to the pelican, also live in profusion on Seymour. With a wingspan of three metres or more, these enormous black birds are most impressive. During courtship, the male who remains on the nest during its construction, develops a pouch in its throat, which inflates into an enormous red balloon. Perhaps this brilliant bulge discourages other frigate birds from stealing sticks from his nest. For the frigate, or man-of-war bird, is a thief. They cannot swim, but due to their amazing agility in the air, are able to harass other sea birds until they drop the food they are carrying. The frigate then promptly catches it in mid flight.

Later in the day we sailed past Santa Cruz once more. Dropping anchor we took to the dinghy and rowed into a shallow mangrove encircled creek. Everywhere swimming under water were turtles one or one and a half metres in length. They were so numerous that we could reach down into the water and touch them. Normally they are timid creatures, but this was their mating ground and they had other things on their minds. Every few moments in that otherwise perfectly silent world, a head would emerge from the water with a gasp for a breath of air.

At 5 a.m. we weighed anchor and set sail on the three and a half hour voyage to the Island of Santiago. Flowing into the sea, as if set in time, was a field of black viscous lava. Once it had flowed slowly like black treacle, but had long since set into wrinkled ridges, showing direction of flow.

We crunched our way up a loose pile of cinders to the top of a dormant volcano. Before us, as far as the eye could discern lay an undulating sea of purple, red, mauve, brown and black cinders. Small cinder cones pock-marked that sterile ocean of desolation.

Near to Santiago is the enchanting Island of Bartholome. We walked up a slope past cinder cones only seven metres or so in width and height. From the top of the hill is one of the most spectacular views I have seen. Two sandy bays lie back to back. Beyond are more cinder cones and a giant wedge of weathered rock pointing skywards, seventy-five metres or so.

If only there were fresh water on the island, I could easily imagine that paradise as the setting for the world's most exclusive hotel, luckily there was no supply of fresh water on any of the islands we sailed to. Consequently they are uninhabited and unspoilt.

Within one of the bays turtles were so numerous that we could see twenty or more at a time in the shallow water. Their tracks led up to the sand-dunes behind the beach, tell-tale evidence of where their eggs were laid.

Scrambling over the rocks at the base of the extraordinary rock spire, we came across a colony of small penguins. One expects to see penguins in the sub-zero temperatures of Antarctica, but not on the Equator. But on the Galapagos, the unexpected seems to be normal, for with a cold current of water from the south, meeting a warm current from the north, the fauna and flora do not seem to follow the conventions of latitude.

With our food supplies depleted by rats, we tried some of the cactus. When skinned it had a cucumber-like texture, but with a peculiar sour taste. However, we did manage to catch a barracuda which, when cooked, turned out to be amazingly tasty.

Before returning to Santa Cruz the following day, we called at the Island of Daphne. The island is really the top of an extinct volcano, which rises so steeply from the water, that landing by dinghy was distinctly tricky. We scrambled on all fours, over loose pumice-stone to the rim of the crater, where a few ghostly white trees and cactus plants were growing. On the level floor of the crater far below, hundreds of boobies were in all stages of nesting, while on the actual rim, there were hundreds more boobies of a different variety.

Cathy and the other Europeans left a couple of days later on the civilian plane, while I still had a week to wait on Santa Cruz, before the military plane was due to leave for the mainland. During that time I visited the nearby Darwin research station. There is a room at the station where young tortoises are segregated according to species and cared for until they are old enough to be returned to their respective islands. Probably fifteen species of tortoises once inhabited the islands, but during the eighteenth and nineteenth centuries, before the days of refrigeration, sailing ships frequently stopped at the islands to take on fresh meat. Tortoises were ideal for this, as they could be stored below deck and kept alive for anything up to eighteen months without food. Consequently there are now only ten species on the islands and some of those are endangered, though now killing tortoises is strictly against the law. But man, by inhabiting the few larger islands, has brought dogs and rats with him, so reducing the chance of survival of eggs and young tortoises. Hence the need to care for tortoises during the early part of their lives.

Also at the research station are paddocks where adult tortoises are kept. Some of them being up to 1.60 metres long. Contrary to popular belief they don't apparently live any longer than the small domestic variety. 100 years old is reasonable, though the eldest tortoise at the station was 160 years old and weighed 270 kilogrammes.

In order to observe tortoises in the wild, I hitched a lift along the island's only road, to Santa Rosa, a collection of four wooden shacks. Away from the coast the higher interior of the island is covered in thick vegetation. Black and lime green moss hung in streamers from the branches of gaunt white twisted trees, around which convolvulus twined. A weird and rather sinister spectacle; no cacti though. With a cloud cover in the centre of the island it is much cooler and obviously enjoys a considerable rainfall. However, much of the natural vegetation has been cleared for banana plantation and grazing for cattle. Despite some of the grass which was as tall as a man, I did manage to locate thirty or more tortoises of various sizes.

As I lay in the loft on what passed for a bed, on my last night on the islands, I found my plastic food bag was being chewed at by numerous mice. I shooed them off and hung the bag from a low beam in the loft. Later in the night I was woken by the scratching of plastic, to see in the dim light a chain of mice hanging on to each other, stretching from the beam to the bag.

The bus took 40 minutes to travel across the island, then there was a ferry to take us across the narrow channel to the island of Baltra. A military bus took us across that island of brown volcanic rock, dry grass and cacti to the airport building.

I was sorry to leave the islands, for besides the natural interest there, I had enjoyed European company. There was a restful feeling of tranquillity and I felt secure, no need to be constantly on the watch for pickpockets and thieves. The first thing I did on returning to Guayaquil, was to take my watch off and put it in an inside pocket, to prevent it being ripped off my wrist.

Knowing that a batch of mail should be awaiting my collection at the post office, I made that my first port of call, but no luck. After a night in the now familiar whore house, I returned to the post office where an employee spent the best part of an hour at my insistence, searching for an expected package of films, but again with no luck. Later when visiting the British Consulate, I was greeted with the most welcome news. After I had left the post office, the man had found the package and realising I was English, had phoned the British Consulate. Yet another person in that city of sin to whom I shall be eternally grateful.

Brazil – On the banks of the River Amazon

Bolivia – Little girls at Chipaya

Bolivia – Pre-Inca statue at Tiahuanaco

Bolivia – Herding sheep at Tiahuanaco

Peru – Reed boat on Lake Titicaca

Peru – Temple of the Sun, Machu-Picchu

Peru – A street in Cuzco

Peru – The ruined fortress of Sacsahuamán

Galapagos – The uninhabited Island of Bartholome

Galapagos – The lava-encrusted Island of Santiago

Chile – The Cristo, symbol of eternal peace

Chile – Laguna del Inca above Los Andes

Chile – The picturesque Laja waterfalls

Chile – Castro waterfront

Chile – Straits of Magellan

Argentina – National Congress building, Buenos Aires

CHAPTER 7

IN TO THE ANDES AND INCA RUINS

The Galapagos visited, it was now my intention to hitch south down the west coast of South America, until I reached — reached where? I really did not know. It was all a matter of how long the money lasted, what the political situation was like when you reach countries yet unvisited, was hitching possible and how far did the road go? In Brazil I had been caught out by roads, marked on my map, which in reality did not exist. Physically, the furthest I could go south was Tierra Del Fuego. It looked an awful long way measured down the map with a dirty thumb. Over 6,200 kilometres as the crow flies and crows don't fly very straight in South America.

Knowing that many new experiences would be waiting for me, wherever I ended up, I walked out of town and stuck out my thumb. While hitching across a hot humid plain of rice, sugar-cane and maize, my attention was caught by a rapid tap tap, as a creature ran literally across the surface of a nearby stream. When it reached the other side I could see that it was a bright green lizard with a black and yellow banded tail.

In the evening I arrived at Cuenca, Ecuador's third largest city. At dawn the following morning, before setting off, I went for a walk down some pleasant cobbled old colonial streets, past the usual Indian markets where local women were already putting up their stalls of bananas, oranges, water melons, bread and a host of other edibles. My wanderings brought me to the central plaza, flanked by the old cathedral. From the ceiling hung a candelabra with 185 lights, the largest one I've ever seen.

Forty-eight hours later and not making very good progress, I arrived at the town of Santa Rosa at 8.30 a.m. There I met the hitch hiker's nightmare. For some unknown reason no vehicles were allowed on the main road. Whenever one ventured to stick its nose out of town, it was immediately turned back by the numerous police who were stationed around. Somewhat bewildered and unable to find out from the locals what was going on, I walked out of town and sat down under an almond tree to crack nuts and await developments. Four hours later the mystery was solved when a racing car drove by at great speed. By the long interludes between each subsequent car I realised that Santa Rosa was on the course of a very lengthy road race.

With no option but to remain where I was, I directed my attention to the ants on whom I seemed to be sitting. There were two distinct varieties, both black, but one group much larger than the other. The smaller variety on observation, seemed in size and instinctive habits to be the same as the common British black ant. However, the larger variety, who mixed freely and without interference with the smaller ones, showed less instinct but a much higher thinking capability and better sense of direction than most. Tantalised with a moving object, such as a twig or a piece of grit, they would observe it for a moment, then according to its size or movements, run away or attack it fiercely.

My experiments helped to pass the time, until 4 p.m. when I saw a military jeep coming along the road. Hopefully I stuck out my thumb; It stopped. The driver led me to believe that he was travelling on urgent military business, but even so it was a bit horrific, driving on a race-track, in the opposite direction to the race. We listened carefully for the sound of engines and when we heard one, promptly drove off the road. I saw one aged sow wander on to the track, then splattered at something in excess of 100 m.p.h. It could just as easily have been an unattended toddler or a horse. Either way it would have been a human life.

My lift thankfully took me off the race-track, then there were no further problems in hitching to the Peruvian border, arriving at 6.5 p.m. Unfortunately that was five minutes after the border closed for the night. Near by was a scruffy shanty village and there I managed to find cheap lodgings for the night. A corrugated iron partition separated me from the pen full of pigs, while near by, deafening music played until 3 a.m., then the cockerels took over. The pigs kept far more civilised hours. They stopped grunting at 10 p.m., though the smell did tend to linger. Still one can't expect everything when the lodgings are cheap.

Hitching free lifts in Peru is not easy, but essential when vast distances have to be covered. Three-quarters of the cars are taxis and practically all the lorries charge. Patience, or the ability to empty one's mind completely, is definitely a virtue, when it is commonplace to wait in the full blaze of the sun, without any shade, for six hours or more at a time.

Three days later, having slept in the desert on the way, I arrived at Lima, just managing to reach the now familiar Pension Union before the midnight curfew. Deserts are such handy places to sleep, as there is no one to disturb you, although sand does lose its heat very quickly and tends to be very cold after sundown.

My next port of call was to be the ancient Inca capital of Cuzco, high in the mountains. This was one place I could not reach by hitching, so two days later at 7.40 a.m. I caught the daily train to Huancayo. For the first four hours the train climbed steadily into the Sierras, zigzagging a total of twenty-two times backwards and forwards up the mountain side.

The scenery at the summit was superb. Snow-capped peaks spilled down red and grey mountains. Broad valleys upholstered with grass, moss, and glaciated lakes spread between rocky crags. I felt quite short of breath, which is not really surprising, for at an altitude of 4,782 metres, it is the highest passenger railway in the world. Built between 1870 and 1893, chiefly by imported Chinese labour, the railway including scores of tunnels and bridges, is a masterpiece of engineering skill. From the summit we began the more gradual descent down the other side, reaching the surprisingly large town of Huancayo at 4.30 p.m.

On enquiring about the next step of the journey, the road to Ayacucho, I was told that it was so rough and narrow, that for 100 kilometres vehicles are not able to pass. Consequently traffic is only allowed to travel north during the day and south at night. I don't like to travel by night and miss the scenery, but there being no choice, I bought a ticket for the 4.30 p.m. bus the following day. It cost me 400 soles, that was equivalent to about £3.50, a lot of money, twice the rail fare from Lima.

There was a clear full moon as we started off from Huancayo and the road, for a mountain road, seemed quite good. Too good to last though. At about midnight it began to rain, the wet season had just begun and the road turned into a sea of mud. The bus slithered on for another three hours, until we finally slid off the road, luckily not over the edge, but into a ditch. There was nothing to do except sit on the bus and try and sleep, while it continued to pour down outside. At dawn we all set to and dug the bus out of the ditch, then with feet sliding, pushed it up the hill. From then on, with the back of the bus frequently slithering across the road, the driver cautiously drove on to Ayacucho, arriving at noon, seven hours behind schedule.

The country we passed through was delightfully pleasant, though typical of much that I had seen in the mountains. Grey rocky mountain slopes speckled with cacti, bushes and eucalyptus trees. Where the land was cultivated there were dry stone walls and one or two roomed stone farmhouses with red tiled roofs.

At Ayacucho I shared a room with Jim and Nina, a North American couple I met on the bus, then together, we caught the 10 a.m. bus the following morning for Cuzco. At 650 soles, I was beginning to think my detour to Cuzco was going to be rather expensive.

The road took us up through grass covered mountains, where for the first time I saw vicuna grazing, then on through mountainous farmland with splendid glimpses of jagged snow-capped peaks in the background.

Spasmodic dysentery had already taken its toll. My belt had gone up three holes, even my watch strap had gone up a notch. That day with dysentery, stomach cramp and a broken wooden seat to sit on, travelling for twenty-seven hours along a bumpy road, was not an experience I wish to repeat.

None too soon and only three hours late, we descended into the flat fertile Cuzco plain, then on into the city. Naked new-born rats squirmed about in a pile of rubbish, as I clattered my way down one of many steep cobbled lanes which lead to the centre of the city. Narrow lanes, shaded by tall ancient stone walls and old houses with lime washed plaster flaking off from beneath their mellow red tiled roofs.

From this labyrinth of timeless picturesque serenity, I emerged into the sunlight of the Plaza de Armas. Now visited by peaceful tourists, it was once the centre of the Inca empire, for centuries the scene of much drama and countless executions. It was here on feast days that the Incas brought out their mummies from the Temple of the Sun and arranged them in rows alongside the ruling Inca.

The early seventeenth century cathedral dominates the square, but more intriguing to me were the narrow roads, built before wheeled vehicles were thought of. Many of the roads are flanked by superb Inca stonework, upon which colonial buildings have been constructed. Granite blocks, some a tonne or more in weight fit together with such unbelievable precision, that a slip of paper cannot be inserted between them. It is not as if the faces of the stones had been cut flat, they are all irregular. Near the cathedral is a large block showing twelve different angles around its edge and yet still all its neighbours fit precisely. Some of the stones have been prised apart by frequent earthquakes, the most violent for 300 years being in 1950. Looking into such cracks it is possible to see that the polished faces fit not only at the exterior but the whole depth of the stone. Regardless of its curvature, its neighbour fits the 'mould'.

Not far from the main plaza is the Temple to the Sun. The stonework, which is considered to be the finest in Peru, so probably in the world, is circular, inclining towards the centre. Consequently during centuries of earthquakes, the stones have remained in, or returned to, their original positions.

On the walls of the Temple to the Sun, the church of Santo Domingo was built in the seventeenth century. Inside I found it to be the most beautiful church I had seen in South America. Very simple, if it were not for the host of pictures which seem so commonplace in Latin American churches.

On the outskirts of Cuzco, on a hill overlooking the city is the ruined fortress of Sacsahuamán. Some of the asymmetrical jointed stones of the bastions are immense, weighing up to an estimated 300 tonnes each. The perfect positioning of those massive blocks still defies belief. What is perhaps more remarkable is that those enormous stones were brought from quarries located thirty-five kilometres away, on the other side of a mountain range and deep river gorge.

Beneath the twenty-one bastions is the parade ground, which is overlooked by a stone seat carved from the solid rock, where the Inca sat while reviewing his troops.

Near by is a gigantic rock, presumably meant for the fortifications, but abandoned just a few hundred metres away from them. In to it are carved, with precision, steps, platforms and holes. Perhaps the transportation was interrupted by an earthquake, for the rock is now upside down. What is mind-shattering, is how the rock was ever moved at all in the first place, for it weighs an estimated 20,000 tonnes. I find it hard to believe that that rock, the size of a large house, could even be moved with the most sophisticated modern machinery.

Two days after arriving in Cuzco, I caught the 1.30 p.m. train for Machu-Picchu, along with Jim and Nina, with whom I had been sharing a room. At the station we could not buy second class tickets as the compartments were full up, for forty pence extra and for the first time in my life, I travelled first class. Though not so appalling as second class, the conditions were still pretty grim.

The train chuffed its way down a pleasant river valley, between little fields of maize. Small thatched dry stone walled huts were scattered haphazardly amongst the fields and everywhere was a profusion of yellow broom blossom. As we went further down the valley the sides became sheer or nearly so and the landscape changed from that of a serene agricultural scene to one of thick jungle.

At 5.30 p.m. the train stopped at the station alongside the Vilcanota river and the three of us began the ascent to the Inca ruins. The track became steeper, until we were clambering on hands and knees up the bed of a stream, hemmed in by dense jungle. Small begonias blossomed among the verdant growth while the tracks of a puma showed up in the slippery mud.

An hour later, muddy and exhausted, we crawled out of the jungle to be confronted by the luxury state tourist hotel and a sign informing us that if we camped amongst the ruins we would be arrested. Needless to say, the way we approached Machu-Picchu is not the way the majority of the tourists reach Peru's finest archaeological site. Buses carry visitors from the station to the hotel, by way of a road which zigzags up the steeply forested mountain side.

The only suitable flat area to be found was about two metres square and directly in front of the hotel. Here Jim and Nina pitched their tent. We half expected to be moved on by the hotel management, but luckily were not.

At dawn, as the mist rose from the valleys, up the sides of the mountains, we entered the deserted ruins of Machu-Picchu. The city at an altitude of 2,280 metres, straddles a mountainous saddle totally hidden from anyone below. Looking out over jungle-covered peaks and ravines in all directions, it is not surprising that the city remained undiscovered until 1911, when a North American, Hiram Bingham, was taken there by local Peruvian Indians.

After the conquest of Peru by Pizarro, the Spaniards were aware that somewhere in the jungle there was an Inca city. They searched for it in vain, although it is thought that it was occupied until the beginning of the seventeenth century. Then apparently, and for what reason we do not know, the city was abandoned. The only fact we do know, which might be a clue to the mystery, is in itself a mystery. After the discovery of Machu-Picchu, archaeologists found that out of all the skeletons which were unearthed, 90% of them were female. The Inca Pachacutec is reputed to have had the city built during the first half of the fifteenth century. In view of the skeletal evidence, perhaps it was constructed as a convent for the Virgins of the Sun, a select group of women chosen from the empire's nobility, whose lives were dedicated to religious services and who were ocasionally offered as sacrifices.

On the mountainous saddle are the remains of stone staircases, temples, palaces, towers and fountains. Spilling over the edge and down the mountain slopes are the inevitable stone-walled terraces of which the Incas seemed so fond.

At the centre of the complex is the Temple of the Sun. This is a circular building with its walls inclined towards the centre, making the construction less susceptible to earthquake damage. Inside is a rock altar, presumably used to celebrate religious rites and offer sacrifices.

Underneath the temple is a cavern, which was undoubtedly a tomb dedicated to nobles. During the excavations, remains of mummies were found there adorned with objects of gold and silver.

Amongst the ruins there are various strangely carved rocks, for sacrifices or ritually drying mummies, but probably the strangest of all is the Intihuatana. In the Quechua language it means 'place where the sun is fastened'. This strangely shaped stone set at a point overlooking the city incorporates a vertical angulated column of stone. The corners of this stone point exactly to the four cardinal points of the compass. The Incas possessed a sophisticated knowledge of astronomy and it is thought that besides being used as a sundial, it was also used as a solar observatory, to study the movements of the sun, moon, stars and the change of seasons.

At 11 a.m. floods of visitors from the tourist train arrived, spoiling the magic of that superb location. At one end of the city the steep mountain of Huayna Picchu (young mountain), rises dramatically skywards. To avoid the influx of visitors we clambered up a steep track to the top of this peak, which once served as a look-out post.

By 2 p.m., we returned to the station to catch the train back. The ticket seller did not want to sell us any, as he said the train was full up. We could see that that was not true, the real reason being that he wanted us to go on the far more expensive tourist train which left at 4 p.m. There are two types of train which run from Cuzco on the 110 kilometre journey to Machu-Picchu. The one on which we travelled was the rather shabby, over-crowded, usually late train which conveys the local Indians and their intriguingly varied belongings. The other, which is several times more costly, runs daily on time, is clean, comfortable and for visitors only. No Indians are allowed on that train.

I left the train at Ollantaitambo, while Jim and Nina continued on to Cuzco. I was sorry to part company, but that is the way with travelling. You meet people you get on well with, travel together and help each other for a few days, then go on your own separate ways.

Ollantaitambo is an Inca or pre Inca village, not a ruin but one which is used and lived in, with certain 'modern' additions of course. The narrow cobbled streets are hemmed in by Inca walls and Inca doorways lead into re-vamped Inca or modern houses.

Just outside the village are flights of terraces leading up to a temple fortress, which contains, like Sacsahuamán, enormous precisely fitting stones. It is here that the Incas successfully repelled Hernando Pizarro and his Spanish army in 1536. Those stones between 150 and 250 tonnes each, were brought from a mountain top ten kilometres away. On the way to Ollantaitambo, somehow, and far beyond our understanding of 'primitive' people, those gigantic, carved, dressed stones were transported across a 300 metre sheer river canyon.

Later in a bar, dimly lit by paraffin lantern (there was no electricity in the village), I met a Frenchman Maurice. He spoke excellent Spanish and had no trouble in finding us a room for the night. The toilet of the house in which we stayed was situated in the corner of a courtyard. It led directly through the wall into a water channel which ran down the side of a narrow street. Fifty metres downstream was where the local women congregated with their buckets to collect drinking water!

The following day Maurice and I hitched a lorry through mountains of lime green grass and wine red rocks, to the village of Pisac. High above the village is yet another Inca fortress, with splendid terraces down the steep hillsides. The climb to the top took us nearly two hours, on the way passing through two areas of fortification, before reaching the fortress proper at the summit. Once back in Pisac and after a lunch of bread and local beer, which closely resembled stout, we hitched a lorry the 32 kilometres back to Cuzco.

There is a road from Cuzco to Arequipa, but it goes up into the mountains where it is cold and carries, I am told, very little traffic. Also as there had recently been much rain, I felt that a dirt road in the mountains might well be impassable. Those were the excuses I told myself but in reality it was my weakness from dysentery and the relatively low fare which made me abandon my principles and succumb to the luxury of a railway carriage.

At 7 a.m. the train left Cuzco and chuffed steadily up a pleasant river valley of maize fields and red tiled adobe farm houses. Beyond the valley the hillsides were dry and scrubby, with occasional clumps of eucalyptus trees. Whenever the train stopped, either at a station, or seemingly in the middle of nowhere, Indians swarmed aboard selling bananas, bread, coffee, cooked meat and chicha, a fermented drink made from maize. Some village stops had their specialities. At one station it would be onions, at another flowers and at the next one maybe hard boiled hens' eggs.

By 1 p.m. we had risen above the altitude for arable agriculture, to sparsely inhabited windswept grasslands, where a few cattle and llamas grazed. The train stopped to refill its water tanks at a bleak spot where hot water was bubbling out of the ground. Quite a large number of the Indians got off the train to walk across and look at this phenomenon. That rather surprised me, as the Indians generally seem so unmoved or uninterested in their environment.

At 2.30 the train reached the top of the pass, at an altitude of 4,314 metres. With snowy peaks quickly receding into the background, the train having laboured uphill for many hours, now accelerated downhill across a bleak windswept plain to the city of Juliaca, arriving four hours later.

I was glad I had not decided to try and hitch. The Cuzco-Juliaca road runs alongside the railway and during the entire day the only vehicles I saw travelling along the narrow dirt road were a bus, a lorry and a bicycle. Only the bicycle was going in the right direction!

After a five hour stop in Juliaca, the train began the seven hour journey to Arequipa, arriving at 6 o'clock in the morning, 23 hours after it started out from Cuzco. The only problem with travelling by train at night, besides not seeing the landscape *en route*, is the risk of having your luggage stolen. Consequently it is advisable to stay awake all night. Not that that was difficult with the hard wooden seats and crush of bodies.

While I was on the Galapagos I had met an English engineer who lived in Arequipa. John worked on an irrigation system to bring water from the Andes, to the desert around the city. As I explained when I visited Arequipa two months previously; it has a superb climate of constant sunshine, but without rain an otherwise fertile plain remains a sandy desert.

As I walked through John's front door that afternoon I immediately found myself cosseted in the unbelievable luxury of an oasis of European life. Cups of tea never tasted so good. Sitting in the soft chair which I couldn't remember doing since leaving England, 'the road' seemed very far away. But two days later after a good English breakfast, it was back on the same road with a long hitch in front of me.

Within an hour and forty miles further on, that oasis of luxury seemed but just a dream. Dropped at a crossroads with not a sign of habitation in sight, just a stony desert with enormous crescent shaped sand-dunes as far as the eye could see. For three hours I crouched by the roadside with the wind howling, sand rasping at my flesh, grating in my mouth, stinging my closed eyes. Sandstorms are not an experience to cherish. But deserts have a magic of their own. Bright yellow wispy clouds streaked a brilliant turquoise sky. As the sun sank to the horizon, the ripples in the sand, casting lengthening shadows, subtly changed through a spectrum of colours. I scooped a hollow in the cooling sand and wriggled into my sleeping bag, glad of the emptiness of the desert where there is no one to hassle you.

CHAPTER 8

CHILE, A COUNTRY OF CONTRAST

Hitching up to, or across borders is always difficult, either because people don't want to wait while you go through the formalities or they feel they might be involved with the police if you turn out to be an undesirable character. At that time there was talk of war between Peru and Chile and I felt that might create additional problems. However, the following day I was lucky enough to obtain a lift with an Argentinian, who took me through the well fortified border post to the Chilean town of Arica.

My first impression of the town was that it was so much cleaner than Peruvian ones, having public rubbish containers. People don't urinate in the street or spit. What was of more vital importance, food was much more costly, though once again I was able to buy milk.

I lost two hours that day, for not only is there an hour change between the two countries, due to longitude, but Chile adheres to the very British idea of 'summer-time'. Not that that makes much difference to travellers who get up and go to bed by the sun.

Another day brought me through a grey gritty desert plain, interspersed with unsightly copper and nitrate mines, to the coastal town of Antofagasta. Sandwiched between the desert and the deep blue sea, Antofagasta is a rather dreary city backed by a shanty town of wooden and tin shacks spreading up the desert hills. However, Antofagasta and its hinterland does enjoy over 4,000 hours of sunshine per year, a climatic phenomenon shared only by Arizona and the eastern Sahara.

It was five days before Christmas. In the central plaza sat a Santa Claus in full regalia. Near by was a clock given to the town in 1910 by the British colony. It was decorated with the Chilean flag and the Union Jack. Chile is by far the most anglicised of the South American countries and there I was to meet many people who spoke English.

Hitching out of town, on a dust cart, I reached the police control post, twenty-two kilometres out in the desert. Here for the first time on my journey I ran into opposition from other hitch hikers. Two singles and four pairs, a depressing sight when there is practically no traffic. But my luck was in and two hours later five of us got a lift in the back of an open lorry. For forty kilometres the road ran in a dead straight line across the gravelly wastes of the Atacama desert, before curving around a hill, then straight again for another forty or more kilometres, disappearing as a perspective pinprick in the distance.

Deserts cool very quickly after sunset and we were all very pleased to have our sleeping bags as the desert changed to lovely shades of pink. At half an hour past midnight, just thirty minutes before curfew, when everyone had to be off the streets, we were dropped off at the town of Chañara. Another rather grim town backed by desert hills, but with the advantage of a vast sandy beach. We hurriedly made our way to it and slept amongst the sand-dunes, hidden away from patrolling police.

'Collectivoes' are common in most of South America. They are cars which travel on certain routes, picking up paying customers. As they are indistinguishable from private cars, it is an additional hazard when hitching. I was most relieved to find that collectivoes were absent in Chile. There were taxis, but as those are coloured black and yellow there was no problem.

For ten hours I stood by the side of the road hitching. One or two cars passed by every hour. After about five hours, the waiting becomes most depressing, but as I waited a woman came out of an old wooden café and gave me a cheese sandwich. Such hospitality goes a long way towards cheering up the traveller, whose worst enemy can be his own over-active mind.

Just as I was in the act of repairing my boots with some wire I had found on the road, a lorry with two Chilean hitch hikers aboard stopped for me. Arriving at the town of Copiapó the three of us found a football pitch. As it was dark we felt that there would be less chance of human excrement there than elsewhere. I slept in the goal mouth where it was sandy, while the two Chileans in true colourful South American style, slung their hammocks from the crossbeam of the goalposts.

Up at dawn and within ten minutes a car stopped for me. One day a ten hour wait, the next, ten minutes. Hitching is totally unpredictable, which in retrospect makes it more fun.

Travelling south the world's driest desert gave way to a covering of stunted bushes and cacti. Two hundred miles south of Copiapó, I saw for the first time, cultivated fields in Chile. Goats nibbled at the impoverished grass between the cactus and bushes. Ragged children stood outside their wooden shacks, holding up home-made cheese for sale to passing motorists.

On the morning of Christmas Eve, a week after leaving Arequipa, I arrived at the fashionable and very pleasant coastal town of Viña del Mar. A little bit of luxury was called for over Christmas, so I booked into the Youth Hostel, which was a dormitory in a sports stadium. I was rather surprised that they were open over Christmas and that they accepted me with a card some years out of date. The cost was equivalent to 25 pence per night and as I had only spent two pounds since arriving in Chile, due to the wonderful hospitality I had received *en route*, I could afford to splash out and buy adequate food for Christmas. It was for that purpose that I made the five mile journey into Valparaiso that afternoon. A pleasant coastal city with a most agreeable climate. The steep narrow streets behind the main commercial centre, with their flights of steps and old buildings, bathed in shadow, have a tranquil Parisian air.

Revelling in the luxury of a bed, I got up at ten o'clock Christmas morning and went to the local park to breakfast on bread, milk and peaches. Then a swim in the sea and on the beach for a Christmas dinner of wine, bread, cheese, bananas and oranges.

After two days of wallowing in undiluted bliss, I hitched to Chile's capital Santiago. Fifty years previously my father had lived and worked in Santiago. I believed that some of his old friends still lived there and I wanted to visit them. Locating them was quite a problem, but to meet and converse with people whose names and exploits I had grown up with, but who I had never previously met, was both strange and nostalgically exciting.

I discovered that one friend I particularly wanted to meet was living in Viña del Mar, so I returned to the hostel at the stadium, only to find that his house was a few minutes' walk away. For four days Jimmy Byrne and his wife entertained me and took me to visit other friends and relatives.

On New Year's Day I was taken to visit another of my father's friends at the coastal resort of Cachagua. Just off shore is a small island on which I was most surprised to see a colony of penguins. It was while swimming near the island that I was caught by an undercurrent and it was with extreme difficulty that I eventually reached the shore, totally exhausted.

Because of the mountainous terrain, the southern third of Chile is devoid of roads. So once a month a ship sails from Puerto Montt to Punta Arenas, the world's southernmost city. Third class tickets for the boat can only be bought from where the ship sails and tend to be sold out many days before departure. Jimmy Byrne felt that he might be able to help me out with that particular problem. His neighbour who owned a shell fish packaging factory in Puerto Montt, offered to ring his manager there, to buy a ticket on my behalf. I accepted, grateful for his help.

Boarding the 2.15 p.m. train for Los Andes, I felt sad to leave the security of Viña del Mar and family friends who I had learned so much about over many years, but who I knew was never likely to see again. After changing trains at Llay Llay (Indian words for wind wind), we slowly chugged along a flat valley surrounded by mountains, bare except for a few scattered bushes. Fruit trees and market gardens seemed to be predominant in the valley, supplying produce for Santiago but eucalyptus and weeping willow trees helped greatly to enhance the landscape. Many horses could be seen working in the fields. The train, much slower and less luxurious than Chilean buses, but much cheaper, arrived at Los Andes station at half-past five.

Charming old horse-drawn victoria taxis creaked along the quiet tree-lined streets, as I walked into town, eating peaches which the ticket collector had kindly given me. Wine seemed to be sold in just about every shop, but I had great difficulty in buying any bread before hitching out of town.

Mv father had often told me of the road from Los Andes which leads right up into the Andes, then beyond into Argentina. I wanted to see for myself what I had been told, and fifty years later nostalgically retrace his steps as far as the Cristo.

The narrow rough road followed the river to the end of the steep sided valley, then by way of thirty hairpin bends, climbed up to Laguna del Inca. The tranquil lake superbly set between towering snow clad rocky peaks, reflects like a mirror the craggy slopes which plunge into its depths. Overlooking the lake is a gloomy fortress of a tourist hotel, a centre for winter sports. A hideous addition to the incredible beauty of nature. I managed to find a fairly sheltered spot amongst the rocks to lay out my sleeping bag, but at an altitude of 2,886 metres, with pockets of snow still visible and a steady wind blowing, I was numb and shivering by morning.

I walked up past the Chilean immigration post, then up to a hideous conglomoration of corrugated sheds, where the 'modern' road and the rack railway disappear into a tunnel bound for Argentina. Until this point, the road and railway are generally in view of each other, both with numerous roofed sections, for avalanches to pass over during the spring thaws.

From near the tunnel entrance the old narrow unpaved road snakes its way steeply out of the end of the valley, up fifty hairpin bends to the Cristo. The Cristo is a large statue of Christ set at the highest point of the La Cumbre pass. It was cast from melted down cannon and erected after the pact of 1902 as a symbol of eternal peace. There is an inscription which reads 'Sooner shall these mountains crumble into dust than Argentines and Chileans break the peace which at the feet of Christ the Redeemer they have sworn to maintain.' But there was not going to be much peace maintained there that day, not as far as I was concerned.

There is a spectacular view, for miles across craggy slopes and snow-capped peaks, of which Cerro Aconcagua, at 6,964 metres, is the highest. In my desire to see as much of the views as possible, I must have inadvertently stepped across the invisible border between the two countries. A Chilean guard came out of his concrete blockhouse and in a fury began emptying my rucksack, throwing my belongings in all directions, which were immediately caught by the howling wind and scattered all over the mountainside. Another guard looked on passively though in agreement with my pleas that such behaviour was not necessary. Nothing would pacify the perverted irate guard, until he had shaken out the very last of my smaller things amongst the rocks and boulders.

By 7 o'clock I had hitched back to Santiago. In order to continue my journey south I caught a bus to San Bernardo, which would take me clear of the city, so that I could continue hitching. While on the bus I fell into conversation with a schoolteacher, who invited me back to his home to stay the night. He and his family were most hospitable and naturally a good meal was most welcome. His wife asked me if I would like a cup of tea. "With milk?" she asked. "Yes," I replied. In due time the tea arrived; boiled milk with a tea bag added! Just one of an infinite variety of ways of making tea in South America.

Tired though I was, there was no chance of getting to bed until the early hours, for the family wanted to practise their English on me and talk politics. Out of all the many people in Chile I met who aired their political opinions, that was the only family who were definitely very much against the military government of the day, looking upon ex-president Allende as something of a martyr and hero. The remark one man made was typical of the general feeling I found in Chile. "You don't know what it was like in the days of Allende. Everything was in short supply. If you saw a queue outside a shop you joined on regardless. It meant the shop had something to sell and we were desperate for food, any sort of food. He used the police for his own ends. Nobody and nothing was safe. His friends and associates roamed the towns and cities, just taking what they wanted and no one seemed able to stop them. Now with the military government, we have peace and security and once again the shops are full. We don't like the curfew at night, but after a breakdown of law and order, it is necessary."

Leaving San Bernardo in the morning, I hitched south through a flat plain between a coastal range of the Andes. After so much desert the countryside looked delightfully green, with maize, wheat and barley growing in the fields. A rather insignificant looking character in a deux chevaux picked me up and invited me back to his house for lunch. With flower pots rattling in the back, we drove through an impressive gateway into a glorious floral courtyard graced with numerous statues. The house was old and decaying, with a history of former grandeur. As my host put it, "Built when Queen Victoria was still at kindergarten."

In hushed silence we entered the large dining-room. Sitting in regal splendour at the head of a beautiful polished Cuban mahogany table, was his mother. I was introduced and acknowledged by a slight bow of the head. A grand chandelier hung from the lofty ceiling. Many beautiful pictures in ornate gilt frames hung on neglected walls. Light shone into the musty room through dirty cracked windows, showing up the threadbare carpet and glinting on the heavy silver cutlery. Frequently during the meal the old lady rang her handbell and a maid came scurrying in with the next of many courses.

Apparently the family had owned 50,000 hectares of farmland, but the Allende government had 'liberated' it. Now they just owned the family home and made a living by growing plants commercially in the extensive landscaped gardens.

That evening, just before curfew, a lorry dropped me in the city of Chillan. Walking out of town with only minutes to hide myself the only place I could find to sleep was a rubbish tip. With rats and mosquitoes and not knowing what you are lying on, it's not the most favoured accommodation.

In the vicinity of Chillan the landscape is not unlike that of England, were it not for the large number of weeping willow trees, the masses of corn-flowers which line the roadsides and of course the Andes which are invariably in the background.

Just a few miles south, on a latitude with Concepcion, I began to enter an area of large forestry plantations, mainly fir. It is here that the Laja falls, one of the most picturesque waterfalls in Chile, is visible from the main road. Needless to say, like many easily accessible points of outstanding natural beauty, it is overlooked by a hotel and restaurant.

A young man who was going to Lake Villarrica for a holiday, gave me a lift and as I still had four days before the appointed time to collect my ticket at Puerto Montt, I went along too. We passed through some of the most lovely pastoral scenery I have ever seen. An undulating landscape of cornfields and tree-shaded cattle pasture. Everywhere, but especially on the roadside verges, an array of wild flowers of all colours seemed to grow. I asked several people the name of one particularly beautiful orange flower which grew in profusion, but no one knew, as far as they were concerned it was just a weed. I had to bring a pressed specimen back to England, in order to find out that they were Peruvian lilies.

On the edge of the lake is the small and rather pleasant town of Villarrica, its wooden houses painted in a variety of colours. From there we drove further on around the lake to the more picturesquely situated, tourist orien-tated town of Pucon. Miquel and I parted company; then soon after, as I was looking into someone's garden at a bush covered in fireflies, three Chilean youths called to me from the house, asking me what I was doing and where I was going. The result being, I was invited into the house and given a meal. Then along with a package of food for my breakfast, they took me to a lovely wooded peninsula and showed me a secluded grassy bank overlooking the lake, where I could spend the night. I lay in my sleeping bag enjoying the balmy evening, thinking of the wonderful hospitality I had enjoyed in Chile. The only food I had bought since leaving Viña del Mar, was one loaf of bread at Los Andes.

In the morning, I washed myself and my clothes in the lake and at 2 o'clock met Miquel, as arranged the previous day. We drove up the gracefully symmetrical steaming Villarrica volcano as far as the snow level. The view of Chile's lake district was most impressive. Three years previously the volcano had erupted, the hot ashes burning the trees stark white, for a radius of about four kilometres. Miquel decided to spend the night at the town of Loncoche. As it was rather late, we had spent several hours fixing a leaking radiator hose and I did not want to be in town at night-time, Miquel dropped me by a bus shelter. Highly desirable accommodation, especially as the entrance was partly hidden by bushes and long grass.

A lorry gave me a lift in the morning, but soon after Loncoche it broke down. Miquel, driving past, saw me standing beside the lorry and stopped to pick me up. We parted finally in the city of Valdivia. Built on a bend of the

Chile – the Villarrica volcano

only navigable river in the country, the setting is superb. Valdivia is a spacious city containing a mixture of old painted wooden houses and modern achitecture. The blend is not unattractive, probably because the city is reasonably prosperous, so can afford to consider appearances.

Passing an ancient and carefully preserved small, round fort, I hitched a lift which took me all the way to Puerto Varas. On the journey, passing through undulating grain and pasture land, numerous bullock carts creaked along the road, many of them with the age old simple wheels made from slices of tree trunk. Once again the hedgerows were ablaze with the colour of foxgloves, vetches, cornflowers and lilies.

Puerto Varas is a small sleeping town on the shore of Lake Llanquihue. Built by German settlers it still preserves its German character and impeccable cleanliness. Overlooking the town from the other side of Chile's largest lake, is the 3,556 metre snow-capped Osorno volcano.

The three Chilean lads I had met in Pucon, had told me of a hostel in Puerto Varas belonging to a religious organisation. On enquiring I found the charge was only seven pesos, less than thirty pence per day. With Puerto Varas being such a delightful town and accommodation so cheap, it was the ideal place to base myself, until the boat left from Puerto Montt.

Two days later, on the appointed day when I was due to collect my reserved ticket from the shipping offices, I hitched the few miles to the rather scruffy fishing port of Puerto Montt. Walking past a shambles of old wooden houses with faded paintwork, I found the offices, only to be told that the boat had been delayed. Instead of only five days to wait, it was now going to be ten. That was bad news, as time means food and food means money. The good news was, at the post office a letter awaited me from Jimmy Byrne, containing the money I had left with him as payment for my passage. Someone else had very kindly paid for my ticket and until this day I have not found out who it was.

With very little to do the next day except explore the surrounding countryside, I hitched off for a day trip to pastures new. An agriculturist on his way to a potato conference stopped for me. He took me out to lunch, during which we discussed the pros and cons of the common and not so common spud. Something one acquires when travelling, to earn one's lift and maybe a meal thrown in now and then, is to be a professional conversationalist,

Chile – Unloading the boats at Angelmo

or perhaps a more apt discription would be, a professional sympathetic listener, as the world is over-full with talkers and sadly lacking in listeners.

Another day, I hitched, or rather walked most of the sixty kilometres along a narrow dirt road to Petrohue. It's not a village but rather a national park, incorporating a number of delightful waterfalls. Then on to the end of the fuchsia lined road, to Lake Todos Los Santos.

Leaving the road I skirted around the lake through the forest, then before me, a landscape of sombre destruction. Old trees twisted and gnarled, stood dead and ghostly white against the sky. Towering behind, as a grim reminder of the destruction, was the Osorno volcano, quietly slumbering until the next time. Through the forest, rivers of volcanic ash snaked their way down the conical slopes to the shore of the lake. Cool now and still, but a grim reminder of the force of nature which cut wide gashes across the country, leaving nothing standing in its wake.

I lay in my sleeping bag on the mossy turf overlooking the emerald green lake. As the day dimmed the sky and lake both turned to steel blue, the snowy peaks, which secluded the lake and me from the outside world, shone pink as they caught the last rays of the sun. The forest was still, just the sound of a few water birds and the gentle lapping of the water on the shore. Then just the water lapping.

Heading back to civilisation the next morning, a Mercedes with a United Nations number-plate stopped when I stuck out my thumb. As the car glided over the pot-holes, one of the family within asked what I would like to drink. After reeling off the long list available, she reached into the cocktail cabinet and poured me out a whisky from a cut glass decanter. If that was not enough of a shock to the system, I was then told that I was being taken out to lunch.

Angelmo is a fishing port tacked on to the end of Puerto Montt. A rather squalid place, but fashionable for its market stalls selling coarse woollen garments and rugs. All hand-made by Indians on the offshore islands. Horses stood knee deep in the water as fishing boats unloaded varied catches into their carts. Then others waiting on the stony beach would take their place, as those with full loads trotted off to the fish market.

A large ark of a boat was permanently moored alongside the quay. This was the spacious and exceedingly luxurious floating restaurant where we dined. With wine freely flowing, we sat down to the most enormous meal at half-past one and rose three hours later after best Havana cigars and brandy. Very much bloated I was then driven back to the hostel. How the rich live and occasionally the lucky hitch hiker.

CHAPTER 9

TIERRA DEL FUEGO

The day for departure came at last and I boarded the boat, having first stocked up with ample bread and cheese to last the voyage. If food was to be supplied, then the ticket was very much more expensive.

The small dark cabin, very overcrowded with six bunks, stank of diesel fumes and putrid bilge slops. Within minutes of settling in, one of my cabin mates, in a very indignant tone, informed an officer that there was a rat in his cabin. The officer, very concerned, inquired which cabin was his. On being told, the officer's classic reply was "Oh! Third class, well what do you expect?" With my food in a polythene bag, dangling from the bunk above, I went to bed fully clothed, rucksack for a pillow, blanket on top of me and one under. Having taken care that the rats would have great difficulty in reaching my food and that my clothes or rucksack could not be stolen, I assumed that I had thought of everything; not so. By three in the morning the bed bugs had managed to burrow through from the filthy mattress and started biting with a vengeance. The next night I took the obvious precaution of putting my polythene sheet over the mattress first, to keep them in their right place.

On the morning of the second day, the *Navarino* arrived at Castro on the island of Chiloé. Here, we were to take on a cargo of potatoes and timber. Much of the island is rough and uncultivated, or woodland. What is farmed is generally devoted to dairy cattle and small fields of potatoes. The houses or shacks, of the Indians or part Indians, are generally small with an air of poverty, the inevitable stove pipes protruding through corrugated iron or wood shingle roofs. Along the coast, many of the colourful timber houses are built on stilts over the water. Dominating the central plaza of Castro is the cathedral. Built of wood, it is covered with corrugated and flat iron, the whole edifice being painted bright orange.

Once loaded, we left Castro and continued south between rugged forested islands, with no sign of habitation until two days later when we anchored off Puerto Eden, the last retreat of the Alacalufe Indians. An armada of rowing boats came out from the small community of wood and corrugated iron huts. Men clambered aboard, selling smoked mussels and enormous crabs. We tucked into a declicious change of diet, while they, with money from their sales, crowded into the bar for their fortnightly booze up. After two hours they were hustled off the ship and somehow rowed home.

Steaming south for two more days to Punta Arenas, in the Magellan Straits, we passed a couple of wrecks, one with its stern sticking out of the water at a very dramatic angle. Rugged mountains plunged into the water on either side, their jagged snow clad peaks disappearing into stormy clouds. Glaciers emerged from within those unimaginable inhospitable regions, to plunge into the sea. This was January, summer-time. I shudder to think what horrors winter holds.

At 6.30 in the morning we were hustled out of bed, so that the ship's blankets could be collected. The company was going to make sure that no one stole any. I went on deck to see gulls mewing in profusion over Punta Arenas, a sprinkling of red, blue and green homes against a bleak moorland background. Across the channel, a golden sunrise over Tierra del Fuego reflected across still steel grey waters.

With rain pouring down, I set off to delve into the mysteries of the world's southernmost city. There was in the city a private museum which I had been told was worthy of a visit. Before long I found myself in the musty hallowed portals of an old, presumably Victorian school. Then after a lengthy wait, my contribution paid, I was led upstairs to a vast room, the museum. Looking at that typical eccentric Victorian collection, I felt as if I had stepped back in time. Even the surroundings oozed a musty, dusty, timeless smell of serenity of a past age. All mixed up and just to name a few, were old photos of missionaries with Patagonian Indians, stuffed condors, an albatross, a dug-out canoe, a wigwam, a penguin feather blanket, an octopus pickled in a jar and a pile of old whale bones. The intriguingly haphazard collection was for me, fascinating.

After that gem of a place, I went to visit the city's public and official museum. Small, modern, well organised and properly labelled, it was very dull in comparison. That is except for one exhibit, the Milaton. During the last century, the bones of an extinct animal were found in a cave on an offshore island. The bones would appear to come from what can best be described as a large bear-like mammal. What is to me fascinating, is that the bones are not fossilised and hair from the animal is still in evidence. Surely if the hair is still in existence, in such a climate, then the remains can not be of a prehistoric age? Looking at the specimen of ginger red hair in the museum and at an artist's impression of what the animal might have looked like, I could not help but think that the colour and form of the animal, were identical to those of the reports of the Yeti of the Himalayas and the Sasquash of North America. Are indeed the Milaton, the Yeti and the Sasquash, one and the same thing?

In the evening, after arranging to sleep on the floor in someone's private house, for the sum of ten pesos, I went along to the British club. The dining-room, billiard hall and the reading room were empty, but full of Edwardian ghosts of a grander age. Perhaps being so British it made me homesick, for I felt a certain sadness in this relic of the past. Once there were over one hundred British born inhabitants in the city, now there were only ten. Selecting an antiquated volume from the library, I sank into a deep padded leather armchair, eager once more to see words written in English. An hour later my solitude was interrupted by the entry of an English family I had met on the boat. They offered to buy me a drink and when the barman finally arrived, I was given the one and only bottle of beer in the bar. Eager for news, I asked the barman, who had worked there for 27 years but still did not speak any English, for a British newspaper. There were none to be had.

At two-thirty the following afternoon, I boarded the ferry for Tierra del Fuego, 'land of fire'. I was told it was given that name by Magellan when he sailed up the channel and saw all the Indians' fires along the shore. For two and a half hours we ploughed through a myriad of sea birds skimming across our bow, or bobbing like countless white dots on the water. Passing a wreck, the ferry with ducks and geese flying overhead, nosed its way up a creek through a barren rain-lashed landscape to Porvenir. It was a quiet town of colourful corrugated iron houses, not unattractive in a bleak frontier sort of way.

Once out of town there was no shelter, no trees, just an inhospitable expanse of short rough grass, herbage and a few odd stunted bushes. An hour later the first vehicle to come along the narrow rough roads, a pick up truck, stopped for me. When he asked where I was going, I replied that I just wished to see the country and maybe visit a man by the name of Mirko Jordan. Jimmy Byrne had been very insistent that should I go to Tierra del Fuego, then I was to call on this friend of his. Many times when travelling I have been told to call in on friends of people I have met. I very rarely do, for to have a complete stranger turn up on your doorstep is a great embarrassment to most people. So I rather surprised myself when I mentioned this man's name, for I did not even know where on the island he lived. The driver asked what I wanted of this man, so I told him my story. Laughing and grinning from ear to ear, he announced that he was Alexandre, Mirko's brother and also a good friend of Jimmy Byrne. At this he insisted on taking me back to his estancia.

For 110 kilometres we rattled along through the bleak countryside, passing the entrances to only seven other farms on the way. Then turning off the road, we bumped our way down the 'drive' for five kilometres to his home, a plain corrugated house, stable, workshop and barn. In the barn were sheepskins, dry salted pork, supplies of human and animal foodstuff and a multitude of other provisions necessary for survival over long periods of isolation, sometimes all winter. As the land is left in a totally wild state, the 4,000 sheep he owns have a free run over as many hectares. By English standards that is a lot of land, but Alexandre assured me that by local standards his was a very small estancia.

After showing me around his outbuildings, Alexandre attended to his tethered horses, then we went into the house. Within was a table, some plain wooden chairs and an old white whiskered man cooking half a lamb and some potatoes on a black range. The old man, a Yugoslavian, was Alexandre's only human company. In his youth, he used to work on the whaling ships in the days of sail. That evening, with a full belly and sitting around a wine bottle by the light of a paraffin lantern, the old sailor was induced to recall some of his fascinating past. One of his stories gives an indication of what a bleak wind-swept area Patagonia really is. When he was a boy he had an uncle who was a lighthouse keeper. The wind blew continually for many months, so the supply ship was unable to reach the lighthouse. Consequently, his uncle died of starvation.

In the morning Alexandre drove me over to his brother's estancia. He told me that Mirko's land, about 10,000 hectares, which supported about 7,000 sheep, was an average sized holding for Tierra del Fuego. I need not have had any fears, for Mirko was delighted to see me, inviting me to stay as long as I wished. So often I find that hospitality increases in geometric progression to one's distance from civilisation. Even the dogs were friendly, when everywhere else in South America they were most aggressive. Without exception they wagged their tails in greeting. But then they are not trained to defend property, there is no need. There is an Arabic saying, 'the desert breeds men'. I feel that that must be true of many isolated districts. Trees in a jungle distort themselves in their fight for survival. The perfect tree must stand alone, free to develop without hindrance, likewise man. The Jordan brothers confirmed my philosophy. They were not empty voids waiting to be spoon fed by outside stimuli. Mirko in his seventies, was still highly active in mind and body, knowing that his life-style was supreme. Aware that he lived in a glorious place where he was his own master, free of any mental or physical domination. A happy content man who can live with himself and his thoughts.

Eight men along with their horses, about twenty-five, lived on the estancia. But there were no women. In fact outside of the town of Porvenir I saw none at all. The vast wild expanses of rolling grasslands are still very much a man's world. There is nothing but sheep farms, so children have to remain in town for their education.

In the winter the sheep stay near the coast, away from the snow, but now it was summer-time and the sheep had all just been sheared. The men were busy with a machine, packing the wool tightly into bales. Each bale, which holds around eighty fleeces, weighs 250 kilogrammes and is about 1½ metres long by ¾ metre square. The average amount of wool produced annually by a 10,000 hectare farm like Mr Jordan's, is about thirty-five tonnes. Once baled, it is then usually shipped to either England, Germany or Holland.

Walking across country on a fresh sunny day, I stood on the summit of a hill. As far as I could see in any direction there was nothing man-made, not even a fence post. Small wild flowers poked out from amongst the coarse grass and lichens. Bushes stunted by the vicious winter winds, were covered with white daisy like flowers. Flocks of countless wild geese flew overhead, while amongst the rough grass I found their nests made from their own feathers.

After I had been at the estancia for a few days, Mirko had business to attend to on the mainland, so he gave me a lift back to Punta Arenas. His parting remark was, "If you ever want somewhere to come and die, come back to Tierra del Fuego and we can die in peace together."

Walking past a shipping office I noticed a familiar figure inside. It was Maurice, the Frenchman I had met in Ollantaitambo, over six weeks previously. Delighted to see each other again, we embraced in true French fashion in the middle of the office, attracting considerable attention. Maurice had journeyed south through Argentina and was now desperately, but unsuccessfully trying to buy a ticket for the return trip to Puerto Montt. The *Navarino* was due to sail in about two hours' time.

Over a cup of coffee we exchanged travel information and the predicament Maurice found himself in. Having seen the set-up at Puerto Montt, I assured the dispirited Maurice that there was still hope of a passage on the ship. At Puerto Montt, for some unknown reason one or two places had been kept in reserve, then sold off at the last moment. We returned to the shipping office just minutes before the *Navarino* sailed and Maurice obtained the much desired ticket.

Early in the morning I began the long hitch north through Patagonia. The name comes from 'Patagones', or big feet. That was the nickname the Spaniards gave to the native inhabitants in that southern part of the continent. The country was bleak, windswept and cold. Besides the sheep, the only other animals visible were the occasional groups of rheas. Although known as the South American ostrich, the rhea is considerably smaller than its African cousin and lacks its flowing plumage.

Once across the border and rather sad to leave Chile, flat lime green grassland stretched to infinity. Small volcanic cones protruded at intervals from the plain, black against the thunder laden sky.

By evening, after much walking and waiting, I arrived at the hideously unattractive town of Rio Gallegos. Basically modern and functional, it reminded me of the worst kind of North American towns I have seen. The culture shock was that I had arrived in a drab, materialistic, westernised society once again. With a thunderstorm imminent, I was unwilling to sleep in the open, but was dismayed to find that the cost of food and lodging was even higher than in Chile. A bed in a very sleazy bar cost me 700 Argentine pesos. (400 pesos to the pound.)

Bread and water for breakfast, then half the day spent walking slowly across the uninspiring wilderness. But luck was on my side, for at midday I hitched a lift the three hundred odd kilometres to Calafate. Not far out of Rio Gallegos, the minor road west branches off the main highway north. The road surface quickly deteriorated, so much so that it was sometimes preferable to drive across the open prairie than slither through mud and pot-holes. Arriving at a delightful little town just before nightfall, I was now viewing, at a distance, the Andes from the other side.

After a rather cool night in a field, I caught a bus for the 80 kilometre journey to my destination. It was the first time since Santiago that I had caught a bus and I hated doing it, but where I was going was up a narrow dirt road through the hills, with no village at the end of it and precious little chance of a lift for days.

I left the bus by the delightfully wooded shores of Lake Argentino. Across the water and reflecting in it, were the jagged snow-capped peaks of the Andes. Cattle lazily stood in the shade of trees. Insects buzzed in the warm sunshine amongst the meadow flowers. But just in front of me, huge lumps of ice, hundreds of tonnes in weight, were floating in the lake, white and translucent blue in the bright sunshine.

Further around the lake was the Moreno glacier, my destination and reason for the more than 700 kilometre detour from the main road. One of South America's most spectacular features, the thirty-five kilometre glacier grinds its way forty centimetres daily from the freezing wastes of the Andes, to end as a wall of jagged ice plunging into the lake. By a few centimetres each year, the Moreno glacier is advancing, while apparently all other glaciers in temperate lands are retreating. With the end of the glacier, a sixty metre high wall of ice, towering above me, the surrounding temperature was distinctly cold. Every few minutes there was a thundering roar as a gigantic chunk of ice broke off the cliff and crashed into the lake, causing waves and spray to dash against the ice worn rocks. The ice cliff stretching for over two kilometres, forks into two adjoining lakes. Dammed by the ice, the level of one lake is 35 metres higher than the other.

By nightfall I was back in Calafate. There walking down the street I saw another individual carrying a rucksack. The result being that Charlie from the USA invited me to share his tent for the night. That solved the accommodation problem.

At dawn I was on the outskirts of the town, hitching back to rejoin the main highway north. Two hours later the first vehicle of the day passed me, the weekly bus to civilisation. I was tempted to catch it, but knew that I could not afford the fare. Now there was no other way out but to hitch.

At one o'clock a car with an Argentinian hitch hiker on board gave me a lift for fifty kilometres. We were dropped in the middle of nowhere, just a rough narrow road stretching into perspective infinity for well over 200 kilometres. Although the sun was shining a cold wind howled across the plain. A green, red and yellow sheen rippled along the roadside, as small feathery grass like bushes were buffeted by the wind. For hours we stumbled on hoping to find shelter, the wind actually blowing over my feet. I know my boots were in a bad way, but that was ridiculous! The story the old sailor told me about his uncle dying of starvation in a lighthouse came back to me, with a much greater personal understanding.

Five hours later we saw a streak of dust blowing in the wind behind us. Minutes later a vehicle appeared as a pinprick in the distance. Roberto and I flagged him down. So for forty kilometres we rode in the back of a breakdown truck, until he turned off down a track.

Just before nightfall we spied a farmhouse set way back off the road, the first house for sixty kilometres. Since Calafate we had seen not a single sheep or cow, only a few wild guanacos in that vast wilderness. We knocked on the door and Roberto asked if we could sleep in the shed. Luckily the farmer agreed and after a very acceptable supper of beans and tea, we thankfully sank into a pile of smelly sheepskins for the night. Our host gave us breakfast of bread and coffee, then it was back on the open road. Two cars passed us as we battled against the wind, but at three in the afternoon, the third one stopped for us and took us all the way back to civilisation, back to the main road.

Now there was considerably more traffic and it was not long before a man and his wife stopped for us. They invited us back to their home in a nearby town to stay. We both gladly accepted and the hospitality was such that very soon not only had we had a shower, but all our spare clothes had been through the washing machine. Then we were sat down to a splendid meal, all the more acceptable because neither of us had been able to buy anything since Calafate and dry bread was all we had left and even that had been rationed.

It was after we had eaten, that our host informed us that he was taking us to the nearby city of Santa Cruz, where we could stay in the airline office where he worked. Puzzled and uncertain about leaving our wet clothes behind, but not wanting to offend our host, we got back in his car. Once at the rather desolate office, he produced a mattress, indicated to us that he also slept there, then just settled down to his paper work.

Left to do nothing but twiddle our thumbs, Roberto and I were rather concerned at the strange turn of events. I have met many strange people while travelling, but have often put it down to the fact that as I do not speak their language, I have misunderstood them. Roberto spoke no English at all, but he had no difficulty in conveying to me that he was also disturbed and thought the man's behaviour most peculiar. At the risk of offending our host, we hitched back to his house to collect our wet clothes. Although his wife gave us a couple of loaves of bread as we left, we felt very relieved to be free of that strange couple. By this time it was dark, but we were fortunate in stopping a lorry going all the way to Comodoro Rivadavia. The lorry was towing a trailer, loaded with yet another lorry. When we pulled into the roadside for the night, Roberto and I slept in its cab.

For most of the next day we travelled across bleak, lonely, windy grassland, grazed by a mere handful of sheep and horses. Cautious of the law, our driver dropped us off before he reached the police post on the outskirts of the city. It was in fact those same police, who later in the afternoon, found us a lift to the city centre.

On reporting to the British Consulate to collect some hoped for mail, I was directed to the local maternity hospital! Surrounded by expectant mothers I asked a nurse for my mail. A masked surgeon emerged from the delivery room and handed me my letters. Mystified by that totally unpredicted comical occurrence, I returned to the Consulate.

The Consul, most hospitably, had invited us both to sleep on the Consulate floor for the night. He then left to go home, telling us that when we went in the morning, to just lock up and put the key in the letter box. It is such unexpected hospitality and trust, which revives one's faith in human nature, making one humble in the presence of such worthy people.

Roberto found some tea bags and announced that he was going to make us both a cup of tea. I relaxed in a chair awaiting the unexpected treat, but being South America I should have known better. What I got was a mug of cold water in which a tea bag was floating. To warm it up Roberto had added some of the Consul's whisky!

After dropping the key in the letter box as arranged and stocking up on bread and cheese, we walked to the outskirts of the oil town. All day we hitched no more than twenty-five kilometres, which was most depressing and probably the start of tension between the two of us. Although we could not converse beyond the basics, we had got along well together, both sharing a similar sense of humour. With Roberto speaking the language, it made life so much easier for me, but I was beginning to feel a loss of freedom or independence.

That evening with an open sided shed to sleep in, the rain lashing down and a cold wind blowing, we lit a fire and I introduced Roberto to tea, English style.

Next day we were more fortunate and by nightfall reached the outskirts of Trelew. We had been led to believe that the police in that area were particularly hostile towards bearded men with rucksacks, a sure sign that one is a subversive Soviet. I had already met other travellers in Argentina, who had been locked up for 24 hours while their documents were checked out for forgeries. Apparently the hospitality during the time of imprisonment had been less than cordial, often with money missing when belongings were returned on release. Although hungry, we dare not pass the police checkpoint in search of food and shelter. Walking in the mud through the shanty town outskirts of the city, we despaired of finding refuge from the cold wind and prying eyes.

CHAPTER 10

HOSPITALITY ON THE HOMEWARD STRETCH

Suddenly out of the gloom some dogs came bounding towards us, snarling ferociously. A man on hearing the commotion emerged from a doorway. One word of command and the dogs became as meek as lambs and trotted back to their master. Roberto asked him if he knew of anywhere where we could stay. Immediately he invited us into his home, an invitation we accepted, but were initially a little wary of, due to the dogs and appalling squalor of the area.

We entered a very small two roomed concrete box, dimly lit by a single paraffin lamp. A rough home-made table and chairs stood in the centre of the room. Pots, pans and tin mugs and plates rested on an old wooden box by the smoke blackened wood stove. A scythe, pitchfork and general assortment of agricultural tools were propped against the walls.

The man, unassuming and quietly spoken, introduced us to his nine-year-old son and daughter of six. It appeared that he had no wife, his daughter attending to all the cooking, washing and cleaning, while his son helped him in his work as a farm labourer. His daughter acted as a perfect hostess and cooked us all a meal of potato soup. The family was obviously desperately poor, so we were only too pleased to be able to offer our stale bread as a contribution to the meal, wishing we had more.

From the other room, rush mats were brought out for Roberto and I to sleep on. I suspect that those mats were their bedding and that that night the family slept on the bare earth floor.

After a breakfast of tea and bread, Roberto tried to persuade our host to accept some money for our night's lodgings, but he would not hear of it. Never before or since have I seen such wonderfully well behaved children. We left that quietly dignified man and his delightful family feeling tremendously impressed and very humble.

Once back on the road, a hearse stopped and gave us a lift to Puerto Madryn. It was at this port in 1865, that over a hundred Welsh immigrants landed. From then until 1911, many more arrived to create a Welsh colony in the vicinity. Welsh names such as Jones and Evans were in evidence on shop fronts and painted on the sides of commercial vehicles, but when I tried greeting the inhabitants in the Welsh language, I got no response.

Near the town and bulging out into the sea is the Valdes peninsula.

At Punta Norte, 160 kilometres away at the far end of the peninsula, is a colony of sea elephants, which Roberto and I thought worth a visit.

Outside the town we waited by the rough narrow road, one car passing about every hour. Without a word, Roberto suddenly picked up his bag and moved fifty metres further up the road. Not knowing what to say I said nothing. Being in such close proximity to one person for a week, had been increasingly getting on my nerves and I expect he felt the same. With lifts so hard to come by, no doubt he felt as I did, that it would be easier to hitch alone. Ironically, a few minutes after he moved and before I had decided what I was going to say to him, a car stopped for me, so we parted company without a word.

The family who gave me the lift, were like me, travelling as tourists to the 'north point'. But to break their journey they were to stay at the peninsula's one and only village, Puerto Piramides. As there was precious little traffic and hitching is difficult enough in Argentinia anyhow, I was very relieved when they offered to meet me the following day and take me the rest of the way.

I lay in the sand-dunes above the tiny village, feasting on bread, cheese, sardines and milk, happy to be once more on my own, though grieved that our parting had been so abrupt. More than 1,100 kilometres north of Tierra del Fuego, the weather was now much warmer. In the sun the sand was beautifully warm, but even so, as soon as the sun set I felt a cold chill seep through my sleeping bag.

Sea elephants are monstrous fat creatures which grow to five or six metres in length. They are elephant grey in colour and seal-like in shape. The head is different though, in that they have a short trunk-like snout. I watched fascinated as a dozen or more lay on the beach dozing, periodically showering pebbles over themselves with their flippers, presumably to cool their fat blubbery bodies. Looking closer at one of those cumbersome creatures, it seemed quite content as long as I did not get between it and the water, but when I did, it erupted and made a dash for the sea. Further down the beach was a separate colony of sea lions and another of sea wolves, — similar to sea lions, but with reddish brown hair and wolf-like faces.

On our way back to Puerto Piramides, where I was eventually dropped, we stopped for a barbecue. Massive steaks were cooked and I was fed until I could eat no more. Several were cooked that were not needed, so I was given the rest to put in my rucksack for later. One day I was eating with a family who could hardly afford to buy bread, then the next I was with a family who had more meat than they knew what to do with!

I had been walking along the road for little more than a minute, when a large, luxury, family car stopped and whisked me north at great speed until sundown. As we drew into a hotel yard north of San Antonio, I presumed my lift had come to an end, but not so. They invited me to sleep in their car, promising to take me further the next day. Unlike the previous nights it was hot, with mosquitoes biting. The cold windy expanses of Patagonia were behind me, I was back to the tropics.

A quick use of the hotel services, with the owner's consent, then back on the road through an endless land of cattle ranches, with innumerable wind-driven water pumps scarring the landscape.

We arrived at Bahia Blanca at seven in the evening, but before dropping me off, my hosts very kindly drove around the city to find out all available information about trains and buses going north. They assured me that now I was approaching the capital, the police would be particularly vigilant and that hitching would be madness.

So hoping for a quiet comfortable ride, as I was paying for it, I bought a ticket for the 9.10 p.m. train to Buenos Aires. Packed like the sardines I was eating, between a boys' baseball team and a troop of girl guides with all their tents, poles and other paraphernalia, there was definitely no room for comfort. It soon became apparent that all seats were reserved and as I had been too late for a reservation, I was ousted to the draughty, noisy space between the carriages for the rest of the night.

It was Sunday morning at 8 o'clock when the train arrived at South America's largest city. Walking along the near deserted streets through a concrete jungle of tall office blocks and shops, I made my way across the grid system of streets and avenues to the centre of the city. The warm morning sun filtered through jacaranda trees, shading the pavement cafés which were just beginning to open. Without the weekday bustle, the narrower streets had a Parisian air about them. But I could not afford to stay in an expensive city like Buenos Aires. Besides, as a foreigner I felt ill at ease over the police witch-hunt for subversive Soviets. I did not want to be involved, and to linger would be to tempt providence.

Catching a bus across the city to another station, I bought a ticket for the midday train to Rosario. Just outside the station in one of the city's numerous parks, is a clock tower given to Beunos Aires by the British residents in 1910. The British seemed rather keen on giving away clock towers in South America. Perhaps it was a vain attempt to shake the inhabitants out of their attitude that 'tomorrow is the busiest day of the year'. If a South American wants to arrange a meeting for a particular time and he means the exact time he says, then it is still the custom to add the phrase, 'Hora Ingles' (English hour).

For six hours the train rattled across the flat pampa, stopping at numerous tiny stations on the way. Beef cattle were still much in evidence. Sunflower seeds, potatoes and maize seemed to be the main crops, though a lot of the land was left to weeds and wasted.

From Rosario, the railway runs north to Sante Fé, but the next train was not due to leave until 3 o'clock the next morning. Wanting to save a night's lodgings I sat it out on a stone bench, until the train eventually left at half-past five.

Arriving at Paraná on the midday bus from Santa Fé, I felt that I was now at a safe enough distance from Beunos Aires to begin hitching again. But even so, at the police post on the outskirts of the town, they searched me and my rucksak thoroughly. However, they did allow me to walk on and hitch.

Rain lashed against the windscreen of the lorry, the road flooded in parts by the nearby Paraná river. But the flat countryside, lower than the road, was submerged as far as the eye could see. Hundreds if not thousands of thatched mud homes were dissolving in the water.

Sitting in the warm cab peering out into the rain soaked darkness, I noticed that at a fork in the road we took the narrower of the two. The driver assured me that we were going in the right direction, though I was unsure, but the dreadful conditions outside persuaded me to stay in the dry cab. The 400 kilometre lift left me at a village and then I knew that although I was heading in the right direction, I was definitely not on the best road, but at least there were lodgings to be had to escape the storm.

Outside every house or church was a hitching rail. Gauchos from the cattle ranches were much in evidence, but everyone else also seemed to be riding along the muddy road on horses, generally bareback. A delightful scene, unchanged for a hundred years, but a nightmare for the hitch hiker.

After being interrogated by the police yet again, a procedure which happened daily while I remained in Argentina, a car did eventually come by, taking me fifty kilometres deeper into the sparsely inhabited swamplands. Blue swamps surrounded by trees and lush grass as far as the eye can see looks delightful on a photograph, but then you don't experience the intense humidity and swarms of biting insects.

First stamping on the ground in an increasing spiral to scare away unwanted snakes, I crawled into my sleeping bag and mosquito net. It was stifling hot and humid in the long grass by the roadside. Frogs croaked in the twilight. Insects bombarded my mosquito net, the smaller ants managing to filter through.

At sunrise the mosquitoes returned to the surrounding marshes. The rutted mud road dried out and cracked in the blazing sun. Standing back from the road were palm trees with green parrots flitting about in the cool shade, but there was no shade by the roadside as I waited for hour after hour.

To maintain sanity I emptied my mind, thinking only of the bite of dry bread and the one mouthful of water I rationed myself to every hour. By the anthills in the road I knew there would be precious little traffic, so after some deliberation I came to the conclusion that should there be a bus, I would lash out and catch it. My hopes were dashed though, when on asking a passing gaucho he told me there wasn't one. I should have walked on, but lack of adequate food made me weak. The hot humidity makes one lethargic and to walk after sundown is to become host to countless blood-sucking insects.

For two days I sat by that road, the sun boring into my head, struggling to keep my thoughts in proportion, so as not to become delirious. That part of Argentina is known as Mesopotamia. According to the Scriptures, life began in the biblical Mesopotamia; I was beginning to feel my life was going to end in this one. But then just as the sun was about to set, a truck rattled down the road and stopped for me. It was the greatest relief to me when we reached the main road once more.

The following day after a variety of short lifts, I arrived at the town of Puerto Iguazu. It rained hard that day, the water swilling in and out of my boots. The red earth alongside the road turned to thick clay mud. The soil is dust in dry weather, which sticks to sweating bodies when vehicles go past, then mud when it rains. Keeping reasonably clean to appear presentable to drivers, is nigh impossible.

Pine trees are grown for paper pulp and tea which is exported mainly to England. But also bordering the road are miles of virgin forest, with the same green parrots flitting about in the gloom. Deep within are jaguars, tapirs, multitudinous stinging insects and snakes. As I walked into the town a car passed towing an immense green snake on a rope.

After a night in a half-built house, upstairs of course, away from any foraging fauna, a car of 1920 vintage, uncluttered by such luxuries as a body or floorboards, gave me a lift for the 22 kilometres to the Iguazu waterfalls, the meeting point of Argentinia, Paraguay and Brazil.

The river Iguazu (Great Waters), falls sixty metres, as scores of cataracts plunging thunderously from rocky ledges, down into virgin forest. The mist from the 275 separate falls forms an array of blazing rainbows along the four kilometres frontage. Walking on catwalks through the dense watery jungle, bright orchids stood out from the verdant growth, while countless multi-coloured tropical butterflies flitted in and out of the gloom. The roar of the water was deafening. Standing on an outcrop of rock, water thundering by into an abyss of spray, the ground literally trembled beneath me. The falls, irregular and in tiers, with the backdrop of rock, wooded islets and jungle, is impressive beyond belief.

Having visited Iguazu, Mrs Roosevelt, then widow of the late US President, wrote in her hotel visitor's book, 'My poor Niagara!'

Just a small outboard motor boat crosses the river at Puerto Iguazu. Then there was a short bus ride to the town of Foz do Iguacu. On the bus two men began to fight and had to be separated. Had I not been in Brazil before, I should have been concerned as to what I had let myself in for. Now I was back in a land of happy, lively, coffee coloured people. People who dressed in rags and ran about with no shoes on. People who lived amongst piles of rubbish and old car tyres, in squalid shacks alongside muddy roads. I was glad to be back in Brazil, glad of the gaiety, glad of the freedom from constant interrogation from the police.

Two days of hitching brought me through forests, tea, coffee, banana and soya bean plantations, to the teeming skyscraper city of São Paulo. One hour in the world's fastest growing city was quite enough for me. Besides it was growing dark, so I caught a bus to the outskirts of that industrial nightmare, to find a quiet roadside verge on which to spend the night.

Three lifts the next day brought me back to where I had started over six months previously, back to Rio de Jeneiro. The last lift with a Major in the Brazilian air force, took me to an air base on the outskirts of the city. First I took a much needed shower, washing off the accumulation of weeks. Right at the beginning of my trip I had been given a pair of trousers. They had served me well, but now patched over and over again and thoroughly indecent, I threw them away. Now resembling something at least semi-human, I was taken into the officers' mess to be fed, then back to his home in the centre of Rio.

The great annual event in Rio is the carnival, the most spectacular in the world. For three days, or rather four nights, Rio with its more than four million inhabitants erupts into a frenzy of noise and colour.

I arrived on the last day of the carnival. In the evening, leaving my belongings with the Major and his family, I joined the vast crowds which were surging towards the city centre for a last night of gaiety. In front of vast grandstands, organised carnival groups danced and sang in strange and fabulous costumes. Floats paraded along the wide avenues, bright with coloured lights. Thronging the streets were bands, music, singing, drumming, shouting, everywhere gay cheerful noise. Stalls selling food and Coca Cola littered the pavements, while drunks, paralytic, littered the gutters. The city pulsated until seven in the morning, but I couldn't stay awake that long and spent the early hours asleep on a park bench.

My return ticket to England was with Argentinian Airlines, so that afternoon when the airline offices were once more open, I went along to book a flight. The clerk looked at my ticket, then handed it back, calmly telling me that it was out of date. But the ticket I had bought in London was an open ticket, valid for one year! The clerk pointed to the writing, it was in Spanish. When I had bought the ticket I could not speak the language, but now I could. He was right, it was only valid for 28 days. I had been swindled by one of those back street shops selling cut price tickets. "The only thing you can do is buy a new ticket, this one is valueless," I vaguely heard the clerk say as my head still spun from the initial shock. Was I asleep? Was it a nightmare? No, it was not, I was in trouble. With only a few pounds left out of the £400 I had brought with me six months previously, there was no way I could pay the fare home. I was marooned many thousands of miles from home and the prospect looked bleak.

Shattered and confused I left the airline office, desperately trying to find a way out. There was a plane leaving at half-past eleven that night and my greatest desire at the moment was to be on it.

Back at the Major's house the wait seemed endless, then, two hours before the flight was due to leave, he very kindly drove me out to the airport.

There I carefully explained my case to the man at the Argentinian Airlines office. After some deliberation, he explained that in the circumstances they would accept my ticket, but I would have to pay the difference between what mine had cost and the price of a full one. That was indeed a generous concession, which they were under no obligation to make, but I still did not have the money to pay the difference. Then after consultation with his associates, he agreed to let me on the plane, but I would have to pay the difference when I returned to Britain. (On arrival in Britain, incidentally, I was not asked to pay.)

It was with the greatest anticipation that I boarded the plane, though still on tenterhooks in case I should be hauled off at the last moment. With a sigh of relief as the plane left the runway, I sank back into the unfamiliar luxury of an upholstered seat and recalled to mind the 28,000 kilometres I had travelled around South America in just six months. I thought of all the strange and fascinating things I had seen, but most of all, I remembered the many wonderful people I had met along the way, people I shall always remember for their kindness and hospitality. Then, taking off my worn out boots, I lay back and dreamed of home.

Argentina – the Iguazú waterfalls